lonely planet

POC

VALENCIA

TOP EXPERIENCES • LOCAL LIFE

JOHN NOBLE

Contents

Plan Your Trip 4

Iglesia de Santa Catalina (p69)
BORISB17/SHUTTERSTOCK ©

Explore Valencia 39

Worth a Trip

Survival Guide 147

Special Features

Welcome to Valencia

Spain's third-largest city possesses a feelgood factor that others can only envy. With a near-perfect climate, long sandy Mediterranean beaches, a fascinating warren of a historic centre, stunning contemporary architecture, big green spaces, superb restaurants and bars (where Valencians spend a large portion of their lives), low pollution, high life expectancy, vibrant arts and entertainment, and long, long hours of sunshine, what more could you ask?

Centro Histórico (p52)
MAN HURT/SHUTTERSTOCK

Top Experiences

Spend a Day at the Ciudad de las Artes y las Ciencias (p86)

Find the Holy Grail at La Catedral (p56)

Sip Wine and Enjoy the Bustle of the Mercado Central (p60)

ROSSHELEN/SHUTTERSTOCK ©

Leave Your Sins Behind as You Enter La Lonja (p62)

Admire Superb Ceramics in a Sumptuous Palace (p42)

See Spanish Masters in the City's Top Gallery (p110)

Wander the Waters of La Albufera (p140)

AARON CABRAL/SHUTTERSTOCK ©

LARANIK/SHUTTERSTOCK ©

See Fine Art in a Historic Seminary (p44)

Uncover Layers of History at Xàtiva (p144)

DIEGO IOPPOLO/SHUTTERSTOCK ©

JENNY/SHUTTERSTOCK ©

Take in the Views from Sagunto's Hilltop Castle (p142)

Dining Out

Valencia has a fabulous eating culture combining quality local ingredients, pan-Mediterranean influences and modern Spanish techniques. Dining is one of Valencians' great pleasures and pastimes: with so many restaurants and bars you could eat well in a different one every day of the year!

Rice

Valencia is famous for its rice dishes, and not just paellas. The incredible variety bursts with all sorts of ingredients from turnips to snails to lobster. Locals are very particular about them, and will judge the quality of the *socarrat* crust as if it were a vintage wine.

Tapas

Valencia has a thriving tapas culture and high-quality tapas. Locals sit and order tapas at tables – often plates, not nibbles – so many 'tapas bars' feel more like a restaurant than a bar.

Where to Eat

Main eating zones are the Barrio del Carmen, L'Eixample and vibrant tapas-packed Russafa. El Cabanyal near the port is on the way up.

The Huerta

Valencia is surrounded by its *huerta*, a fertile plain filled with market gardens irrigated by an ingenious system of channels devised by the Moors. A source of great pride to Valencians, the *huerta* supplies the city with delightfully fresh produce, especially vegetables, citrus fruit and rice.

Best Dining

El Poblet Top-notch gastronomy at Quique Dacosta's place. (p48)

Ricard Camarena Stunning modern cuisine from the city's foremost chef. (p116)

2 Estaciones Two-chef team produces wonders from an open kitchen. (p101)

Rausell Beloved bar/restaurant with fabulous seafood, meat and rices. (p133)

Refugio Pleasing fusion food at sharp prices. (p79)

Gran Azul Superb seafood and steaks in a spacious and elegant grill. (p116)

BODIAPHVIDEO/SHUTTERSTOCK ©

Navarro Brilliant spot for rice that's been going for generations. (p48)

Bar Ricardo Valencian classic with professional service and glorious food. (p134)

Best Tapas

Bodega Casa Montaña Ultra-characterful old bodega with sensational seafood tapas. (p123)

Canalla Bistro Playful fusion from a famous chef. (p101)

Bar Cabanyal Youthful venue for excellent seafood flavours. (p125)

El Rodamón de Russafa Global tapas journey. (p99)

Cervecería Maipi Traditional Russafa tapas bar. (p101)

Best Vegetarian & Vegan

La Casa Viva Russafa locale for creative veggie and vegan fare. (p102)

Copenhagen Cheerful central Russafa spot. (p102)

Las Lunas Great lunch menu with a daily vegan choice. (p91)

Almalibre Açaí House Brazilian wonder-fruit bowls and more healthy fare. (p81)

Spanish Stomach Clocks

Valencians habitually consume huge elevenses called *almuerzo* (*esmorzaret* in *valenciano*). Restaurants typically open for lunch proper from 1pm to 3.30pm. Dinner is 8pm to 10.30pm but restaurants rarely fill before 9pm. After a big lunch (often the case) many people share tapas later. Rice dishes are only eaten at lunch.

Bar Open

Valencia has a vibrant nightlife and bars buzz on weekend and summer evenings. The Barrio del Carmen, quiet midweek, comes to life on weekend nights. Russafa always has an exuberant scene, while students pump the northeast. Meanwhile cafe culture is on the up, with several bright breakfast and speciality-coffee spots.

Barrio del Carmen

The *barrio* is fairly quiet midweek, but its shutters come up on weekend evenings, revealing a starburst of little bars. Decent cafes are easy to find at any time.

Russafa

Russafa has the best bar scene, with a huge range of everything from family-friendly cultural cafes to quirky bars, and a couple of big clubs. On weekend and summer evenings, almost every street intersection seems to be surrounded by overflowing bars and restaurants.

The Northeast

The university area, especially around Avenidas de Aragón and Blasco Ibáñez, has enough bars and *discotecas* to keep you busy all night. It's not just students; this is the city's main nightclub area at weekends. Thursday is traditionally the night students head out to get hammered. Benimaclet has some less frenetic alternative options.

Best Bars

La Fábrica de Hielo A bit of everything at this artsy-bohemian spot near the sea. (p128)

Café Negrito Great, socially aware cafe-bar on a tucked-away square. (p70)

Café Madrid Elegant old-town cocktail bar. (p49)

Tyris on Tap Excellent microbrewed beer in a trendily industrial setting. (p70)

Sant Jaume Pocket-sized bar with a great people-watching terrace. (p70)

Beers & Travels Convivial dark wood craft-beer pub. (p81)

Café Museu A landmark bohemian local bar in the heart of the Barrio del Carmen. (p81)

VTT STUDIO/SHUTTERSTOCK ©

L'Ermità Laneway Carmen bar with a cosy interior and good music. (p81)

Kaf Café Exemplar of the alternative cultural vibe of Benimaclet. (p113)

La Casa de la Mar Sip on a cold one as you enjoy the live music and surfer vibe. (p128)

Café de las Horas An extravagant baroque interior makes this a characterful venue for a drink. (p70)

Angolo Divino Cosy wine bar on a L'Eixample corner. (p94)

Best Cafes

La Más Bonita Perfect breakfast cafe at Patacona beach. (p126)

Bluebell Coffee Probably the best coffee in town, roasted by women in Valencia. (p104)

Dulce de Leche This cafe's baked goods display is impossible to walk past; it has a Russafa branch too. (p48)

Mestizo Delightfully tranquil cafe on a Carmen backstreet. (p79)

Federal Classic international-style brunch-and-laptop hangout. (p48)

Ubik Café Cosy Russafa cafe, bar and bookshop that makes a comfy spot to lurk. (p104)

Best Clubs

L'Umbracle Terraza/Mya Alfresco drinking in an amazing setting plus a club downstairs. (p94)

Radio City Old-town stalwart with a lively, eclectic crowd and DJs or live music every night. (p70)

Marina Beach Club Phenomenally popular bar and club right on the water. (p128)

Piccadilly Downtown Club Appealing Russafa option for some dance-floor action. (p99)

Deseo 54 A mixed young crowd at this popular *discoteca*. (p118)

Rumbo 144 Late-opening student favourite in the university district. (p118)

Akuarela Playa One of the main coastal nightclubs driving the pumping summer scene. (p129)

Treasure Hunt

As befits its big-city status, Valencia has great shopping. All of Spain's big-name clothing stores are present, many in great number, but there's also a thriving scene for smaller-scale, locally designed clothing and accessories. Unique pieces, like a Lladró porcelain or a hand-painted fan, can make special souvenirs.

Shopping Central

The southern part of the old city is Valencia's principal commercial zone, with a major department store surrounded by streets packed with a huge range of shopping options. This zone melds into L'Eixample, where the area around the Mercado de Colón is replete with high-end boutiques, delis and other intriguing shops.

Offbeat Shopping

On the fringes of the main areas, you'll find quirkier, offbeat shopping experiences. These include the streets of Russafa (pictured), full of hipster clothing stores, vintage shops or unusual arty boutiques. The old centre, Barrio del Carmen and the streets near the Mercado Central have fascinating smaller shops.

Best Food & Drink

Mercado Central Fabulous central venue for fresh produce. (p60)

Mercat Municipal del Cabanyal Traditional covered market with high-quality comestibles. (p123)

Trufas Martínez Historic chocolate truffles are a city byword. (p95)

Manglano Excellent deli produce and wine in the Mercado de Colón. (p95)

Mercado de Russafa Thriving *barrio* market stacked with fresh produce. (p106)

Best Alternative & Vintage

Madame Mim Excellent destination for vintage clothing and unusual items. (p107)

Vinyl Eye Lovably unusual shop with hundreds of edgy T-shirt designs. (p137)

Santo Spirito Vintage Spacious destination for classic American and British styles. (p82)

Place A creative space with multiple stallholders. (p95)

Paranoid Design your own T-shirt. (p107)

Needles & Pins Floaty skirts, printed shirts and more, from the '40s to the '90s. (p71)

Best Boutiques & Clothing

Seda Beautiful, locally crafted silk items. (p50)

Sombreros Albero Pick up a trilby from these traditional hat-makers. (p50)

Linda Vuela a Rio Top-drawer perfumery sourcing exquisite global scents. (p95)

Madame Bugalú Stylish, sassy women's clothing. (p71)

Pángala Handmade bags with plenty of non-animal products. (p82)

Luna Nera Colourful, original women's clothing and accessories at reasonable prices. (p82)

La Ruta de la Seda Breezy, stylish, eclectic clothes for women. (p51)

Best Gifts & Souvenirs

Lladró Famous local porcelain sculptures. (p50)

Abanicos Carbonell Valencian fans for Valencia fans. (p95)

Simple Intriguing and original collection of quality artisanry from around Spain. (p71)

La Botiga de l'Artesanía Showcases the best of contemporary Valencian craftwork. (p50)

Artesanía Yuste Enchanting hand-painted ceramics in the centre. (p71)

Kowalski Bellas Artes Unusual shop with charmingly eclectic wares. (p106)

Valencia CF Tienda Oficial Shirts, scarves and more from the top local football side. (p51)

Cestería El Globo Basketwork, wooden toys and other surprises. (p50)

Plaza Redonda Several handicrafts stores around one circular plaza. (p51)

Architecture

The rich architectural legacy so characteristic of Mediterranean cities is very much the story in Valencia. Diverse domestic influences combined with flourishing overseas trade to create a dynamic city prone to innovation, from Roman urbanism to Calatrava's caprices via Moorish elegance, Gothic majesty and Modernista swirls.

Modernisme

The local form of the art nouveau or Jugendstil revolution in architecture and design had Barcelona as its base, but was hugely influential in Valencia too. Modernisme added whimsical motifs, often based on nature, to buildings and sought to play with rigid neoclassical ideas of straight lines. Wealthy merchants patronised promising architects and built grand houses in new expansion districts outside the city walls. L'Eixample in Valencia is a treasure trove of such buildings, as you'll see on our themed walking tour (p72).

Calatrava

One of the world's most famous living architects, local boy Santiago Calatrava first achieved renown with his fluid, striking bridges. Their often skeletal design themes were later incorporated into ambitious building projects the world over. His buildings at the Ciudad de las Artes y las Ciencias in his home town are, despite budgeting and other problems, extraordinary by any measure.

Best Gothic, Moorish & More

La Lonja One of the great Gothic civil buildings left, with a stunning main hall. (p62; pictured)

La Catedral The mostly Gothic cathedral dominates the centre of town. (p56)

Torres de Quart One of only two structures remaining from the city wall, this towering gateway is an imposing sight. (p77)

Torres de Serranos Like its sibling Quart, the Serranos gateway would have scared any would-be attackers. (p77)

MASSIMO TODARO/SHUTTERSTOCK

Centro del Carmen Cultura Contemporánea Exhibition space occupying handsome Gothic and Renaissance cloisters. (p78)

Almudín Extraordinary scale and design in this medieval city granary. (p67)

Castillo de Xàtiva Eagle's-nest fortress with sturdy military architecture from a variety of periods. (p144)

Palau de la Generalitat A handsome Gothic palace is the seat of regional government. (p53)

Atarazanas Though much changed over the years, these Gothic shipbuilding warehouses are still impressive. (p123)

Best Baroque, Modernista & Modern

Ciudad de las Artes y las Ciencias Calatrava's complex of futuristic buildings is a stunning testament to his creativity. (p86)

Palacio del Marqués de Dos Aguas Extravagant doesn't even begin to do justice to this outrageously flamboyant rococo mansion. (p42)

Mercado de Colón This stunning Modernista market building is a highlight of the style. (p91)

Mercado Central The vast Modernista central market is still the city's main hub of fresh produce. (p60)

Estación del Norte This train station is a heart-warming Modernista gem, with numerous optimism-filled details. (p47)

Ayuntamiento Handsome neoclassical building dominating the Plaza del Ayuntamiento. (p47)

Institut Valencià d'Art Modern Impressively designed contemporary art gallery. (p77)

Mestalla The steeply-tiered Valencia football stadium is an intimidating arena for visiting teams. (p115)

Iglesia de San Nicolás This recently restored church was originally Gothic but it's the riot of baroque frescoes that makes it special. (p67)

Espai Vert Astonishing 1980s architectural project aimed at rethinking communal living. (p113)

Museums & Galleries

Valencia has a wealth of museums covering its history, industries, festivals and other aspects of life. Several galleries offer an excellent overview of Spanish art across the centuries. Most of these places, many of which are housed in intriguing buildings, are within an easy walk of the centre of town.

Temporary Exhibitions

One of Valencia's real fortes is its large number of spaces for temporary exhibitions. The larger exhibition venues attract some excellent visiting shows, while the endlessly creative local talent may be on display anywhere from cafes to community arts centres.

Best Museums

Museo de las Ciencias Príncipe Felipe This notable modern building houses a super interactive science museum. (p87)

Museo Nacional de Cerámica y Artes Suntuarias Two excellent museums in one: one covers the important Valencian ceramics industry, the other is the building itself that houses it, an extravagantly decorated baroque palace. (p42)

L'Almoina Descend under the old town to see layers of history unfolded before your eyes. (p67)

Museo de la Seda Explore the history of Valencia's famous silk industry in this well-executed modern museum. (p47)

Museo de Historia de Valencia See how Valencia changed through the ages in this romantic brick-vaulted water deposit. (p133)

Museos de Prehistoria & Etnología Two museums in one giant former convent, covering archaeology and, in livelier fashion, changes in Valencian life since the industrial age began. (p77)

Museo Arroz A former rice mill shows you the machinery that processed Valencia's favourite grain. (p123)

Museo Fallero A charming rogue's gallery of the favourite sculpted characters from each year of the Fallas festival. (p91)

Ayuntamiento Within this impressive civic building is a museum with key exhibits from the city's history. (p47)

L'Iber An astonishing collection of toy soldiers makes this a very out-of-the-ordinary visit. (p78)

ANA DEL CASTILLO/SHUTTERSTOCK ©

Best Galleries & Exhibition Spaces

Museo de Bellas Artes Valencia's excellent main art gallery has a strong selection of Spanish paintings. (p110; pictured)

Museo del Patriarca This seminary's collection of Spanish Renaissance art is small but of great quality. (p44)

CaixaForum A spectacular building within the Ciudad de las Artes y las Ciencias, staging diverse art and other exhibitions. (p88)

Institut Valencià d'Art Modern A major contemporary art gallery with a limited but impressive permanent collection and some excellent touring exhibitions. (p77)

Museo Catedral Fine selection of art in the museum within the cathedral itself. (p57)

Almudín A huge 15th-century city granary that houses exhibitions but is worth a visit for the building alone. (p67)

Fundación Bancaja This bank's cultural foundation brings in excellent art exhibitions with free entry a bonus. (p67)

Bombas Gens Attractive conversion of a former pump factory into a space for edgy contemporary art. (p115)

Centro del Carmen Cultura Contemporánea This former monastery is an attractive space for interesting temporary exhibitions. (p78)

Centro de Artesanía Comunitat Valenciana Compact two-room display of very fine Valencian artisanry. (p47)

Centro Cultural La Nau The old university building in the centre of town contains a historic library and several exhibiting spaces. (p47)

Luis Adelantado Stylish, carefully curated contemporary art in a central gallery. (p47)

Atarazanas These Gothic shipyard warehouses near the port make an intriguing venue for temporary exhibitions. (p123)

Sporting Club Russafa Drop by to see what's on in this community-run arts centre. (p101)

Street Art

As you wander Valencia's streets, your gaze is repeatedly grabbed by dramatic, often colourful images livening up the walls. Far beyond mere graffiti, these images may be straightforwardly beautiful or may be edgy creations of obscure meaning. Valencia is a hotbed of urban creativity where the street art is a constant talking point.

Stars of the Streets

Leading street artists are prominent figures in the Valencian cultural landscape. Some (such as Julieta XLF, La Nena Wapa Wapa, Hyuro, Deih, Disneylexya) sign some of their work. Style also helps to identify: Julieta XLF typically paints Japanese-influenced images of girls with closed eyes; Disneylexya's creations might be considered a psychedelic take on pre-Hispanic art. Ubiquitous David de Limón specialises in black figures clad in Daft Punk–like helmets.

Barrio del Carmen

This is Valencia's street-art epicentre, with something arresting round almost every corner. Free Tour Valencia (p29) does an informative street-art tour here. Most celebrated is La Calle de los Colores (Calle Moret) with its sequence of sizeable murals including a much-Instagrammed kissing couple. On a miniature scale is La Casa de los Gatos (Calle del Museo 9): a tiny house frontage at ground level whose minute detail includes a doorway for local felines.

Other Areas

Keep your eyes peeled while wandering round the traditional fishers' neighbourhood El Cabanyal. There's a particularly impressive multi-artist tribute to 20th-century Valencian illustrator José Segrelles at the corner of Calles Gaillart and Rosario. Fashionable, arty Russafa and working-class Benimaclet are further fertile ground for street-art hunters.

FOTOGRAFIABASICA/GETTY IMAGES©

Don't Miss These Valencia Urban Artists

First I must express how important it is for people to visit the streets of this city with their eyes open and observe the great quantity and quality of its urban art, appreciating for themselves the language of these streets and forming their own conclusions. My first key point is a fundamental crew in Valencian urban art: **XLF**, in whose ranks are artists of great quality such as **Deih**, **Julieta**, **Xelon**, **Barbiturikills** y **Vinz**, all pillars of both the artistic and institutional sides of this activity in the city of their birth.

One artist who for me will always stand out, because of his message, power, innovation and conceptual depth, is **Escif**. He was the first artist who truly impacted me when I arrived in Valencia, totally changing my concept of urban art and making me understand that in this city something special was going on.

My studio colleagues, too, are authentic pillars of the Valencian urban scene: **La Nena Wapa** who expresses her visual poetry through stencil and spray, the omnipresent and iconic **David de Limón**, and **Sonic Armada**, a recent arrival like me but with a power and style that is bound to make people talk.

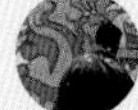

By Disneylexya, *a Chilean urban artist settled in Valencia since 2013*
@disneylexya

For Kids

ROSTISLAV GLINSKY/SHUTTERSTOCK ©

Valencia is an easy place to take the kids, with many experiences for young humans to enjoy. The many apartment rental options provide an alternative to hotel rooms. The beaches are a good attraction, and riding there in the tram is fun. The other great playground, year-round, is the 9km-long park in the Turia riverbed.

Bioparc Innovative zoo that recreates African landscapes and gets you close to the animals. (p133)

Oceanogràfic This massive aquarium with shark tunnel, penguins and more will keep the family spellbound for hours. (p88)

Museo de las Ciencias Príncipe Felipe Hands-on science museum great for all ages, with some areas designed for kids. (p87)

Hemisfèric With a planetarium and IMAX cinema, this is high-approval family entertainment. (p87)

Jardín del Turia 9km traffic-free park with numerous playgrounds. Great for cycling – many bike-hire outfits have kid's bikes. (p115)

Gulliver Unleash the little ones to climb up and slide down this ever-patient recumbent giant (p139; pictured).

Playa de las Arenas The easiest-reached beach, with a lively family scene. (p125)

Valencia Club de Fútbol See one of Spain's biggest football teams. (p118)

Teatro la Estrella Watch enchanting weekend puppet shows in a cute theatre. (p137)

La Albufera Combine a boat trip, beach and birdwatching. (p140)

All-Day Kitchens

Spanish restaurant hours don't always suit visiting kids' body clocks, so all-day kitchens are a godsend. Mercado de Colón (p94) has several options; Bar Ricardo (p134) is a classic tapas bar; or try cafes like Federal (p48), La Más Bonita (p126) and Almalibre Açaí House (p81).

Show Time

Valencia is a hub for the performing arts, with a creative theatre and dance scene and two architecturally and acoustically excellent concert halls. Live music culture in smaller venues is thriving and covers the gamut from flamenco to rock and beyond. The free listings magazine AU (www.au-agenda.com) is handy.

CORRADO BARATTA/SHUTTERSTOCK ©

Palau de les Arts Reina Sofía This stupendous Calatrava building hosts mostly opera, but also classical concerts. (p94)

Radio City Something different on every night in this cultural icon of a bar. (p70)

Jimmy Glass Several gigs a week in one of Spain's top jazz clubs. (p82)

Black Note Popular and well-established venue for live jazz, funk, soul and more. (p119)

Espacio Inestable Tucked away in the northeast of the old town, the edgy 'Unstable Space' has great movement and dance performances. (p70)

La Fábrica de Hielo Large almost-beachside space with a great artsy-bohemian atmosphere and live music several nights weekly plus Sunday lunchtimes. (p128)

La Salà Great live-music nights, with leanings towards world music and local artists. (p118)

Teatro Principal As you might guess from the name, this is one of Valencia's main venues for drama and dance. (p50)

Loco Club A solid program of live music, mostly rock and related genres, from local and touring acts at this reliable venue. (p136)

Café del Duende Valencia's best venue for flamenco; a small, intimate spot. (p136)

Palau de la Música Right on the 'river', the Palace of Music has a top program of mostly classical concerts. (p139)

16 Toneladas By the bus station, this venue has varied live bands (with many international visitors) and is also a nightclub. (p119)

Matisse Club Live music almost nightly, from classical to rock. (p119)

La Casa de la Mar Large lively warehouse near Patacona beach with bands most nights. (p128)

Café Mercedes Jazz Russafa jazz venue with top-notch sound. (p106)

Teatro la Estrella Weekend puppet shows aimed at families. (p137)

Teatre El Musical In El Cabanyal, this impressively contemporary theatre stages regular music and dance alongside its drama program. (p129)

Parks & Outdoor Spaces

LIPSKIY/SHUTTERSTOCK ©

Jardín del Turia The former riverbed is now a superb 9km-long strip of park that gives the whole city a green artery. (p115; pictured)

Ciudad de las Artes y las Ciencias The visual impact as you walk around the precinct, with turquoise lagoons shimmering around the futuristic architecture, stays long in the memory. (p86)

La Albufera A protected *parc natural* of 211 sq km with gorgeous lagoonscapes, undeveloped beaches, birdwatching, rice paddies and walking trails among woodland and dunes. (p140)

Plaza de la Virgen The spiritual heart of the old town, centred on a fountain representing the Río Turia. (p67)

Bioparc An innovative zoo that presents the animals in beautifully landscaped 'African' surroundings. (p133)

Puente de las Flores A riot of flowers covers a bridge across the Turia. (p139)

Jardín Botánico This university-run walled garden is a welcome retreat from the powerful sun. (p133)

Jardines del Real A lovely spot for a stroll, with plenty of palms and oranges in what were once the grounds of a palace. (p115)

Parque Central Abandoned railway yards have remarkably been turned into a landscaped formal park and a green lung for Russafa. (p101)

Playa de las Arenas, Playa de la Malvarrosa, Playa de la Patacona These three city beaches are really one long strip of sand, great for strolling. (p125)

Plaza de la Reina Recently pedestrianised and planted with trees, the square immediately south of the cathedral is now a cheerful open space among the crowded old-town streets. (p53)

Jardín de Monforte Ornamental 19th-century gardens making a peaceful retreat from the city bustle. (p116)

L'Umbracle Terraza Sip a cocktail under the stars at this stylish summer venue. (p94)

Sant Jaume Our favourite spot to sip a drink on a central terrace and watch life go by. (p70)

Parque de Cabecera This landscaped park has lakes, a hill with vistas and ample strolling space. (p139)

LGBTIQ+

INA MUKHUTDINOVA/SHUTTERSTOCK ©

Valencia is a very gay-friendly place, with an extremely relaxed attitude to sexuality. In some ways, that means that there's far less of a separate scene here, with a mix of folk to be expected in any bar or restaurant in Russafa or the Barrio del Carmen, for example. Nevertheless, there are some thriving LGBTIQ+ locales.

Russafa

Russafa is a bustling post-scene locale, testament to the open-minded Valencian attitudes. Friendliness is a given around here and the distinction between LGBTIQ+-friendly and other establishments is so blurred as to usually not exist. This is a fine place to meet people in relaxed pre-club surroundings.

Beaches

Of the city beaches, the northern part of Playa de la Malvarrosa is the most popular. South of Valencia, in La Albufera region, Playa de l'Arbre del Gos is the region's principal gay beach and is spacious, attractive and well frequented by both men and women. It's clothing-optional. You can find it by heading north from El Saler beach or south from Pinedo. Look for a disused chimney stack. Bus 15 reaches Pinedo, while 24 and 25 hit El Saler. From the Carrera del Riu–Coll Vert stop on lines 24 and 25, it's a 400m walk to the beach.

Best LGBTIQ+ Bars

Trapezzio The LGBTIQ+ crowd in the Barrio del Carmen is well established and an important part of the local community. This is a fixture. (p82)

Deseo 54 Young and beautiful people predominate in this nightclub; it's a mixed crowd. (p118)

Planet Valencia A kicking Russafa bar that's lots of fun for lesbians. (p105)

La Boba y el Gato Rancio Casual and relaxed LGBTIQ+-friendly bar and cafe in Russafa. (p105)

Pub Bubu Bears and their friends will find their den here. (p136)

Under the Radar Valencia

PETRAPHOTO/SHUTTERSTOCK ©

The bulk of Valencia's visitors concentrate on the big-ticket sites in the Ciutat Vella, with a trip to the Ciudad de las Artes y las Ciencias added on. But there's a whole lot more to discover, from quirky museums to well-loved local tapas haunts, beyond those areas.

Local Barrios

To get under the skin of Valencia, you can't do better than getting a feel for *barrio* life. While it can still be found in pockets of the old town, it pays to go beyond to the districts where most Valencians live. Here you'll find local cafes and bars, some fabulous places to eat and quirky cultural hubs.

Good areas to begin your exploration are the northern and eastern suburbs (including Benimaclet), the southern stretches of L'Eixample and the west of the city.

Best Under the Radar Valencia

Bombas Gens Former factory converted into intriguing modern arts space. (p115)

Kaf Café Cafe-bar on the edge of Benimaclet that typifies the area's alternative artistic vibe. (p113)

Jardín de Monforte Lovely, little-frequented 19th-century formal garden. (p116; pictured)

Horta Viva Tours and events in the market garden villages that surround the city. (p29)

Museo de Historia de Valencia Off-the-beaten-track museum of city history. (p133)

Splendini Cosy combined bar and secondhand record shop on the fringe of L'Eixample. (p94)

Cantina Monterey Could be just another busy local bar in the Carmen except for its delicious authentic Mexican tacos. (p79)

Espacio Inestable Edgy arts space with sometimes spectacular dance or circus. (p70)

Balansiya Authentic and delicious Moroccan food in a local *barrio*. (p116)

Mestizo In the well-frequented Barrio del Carmen, this peaceful cafe's backstreet location makes it a good find. (p79)

Tours & Courses

SODEL VLADYSLAV/SHUTTERSTOCK ©

Free Tour Valencia (☎961 11 29 01; www.freetourvalencia.com; pay by donation) Walking tours where you pay what you think they're worth. There's a 2½-hour 'essentials' tour (daily from Plaza de la Virgen), a street-art walk and a Modernisme tour.

Mediterranean Surf (☎655 014250; www.mediterraneansurf.com; Avenida Mare Nostrum 7; 2hr class from €28; ⏰10am-8pm Tue-Sun; 👪) Don't expect huge waves in Valencia, but the often-gentle swell and great weather make it a fine place to learn to surf, paddleboard or windsurf.

Passion Bike (☎963 91 93 37; www.passionbike.net; Calle de Serranos 16) Friendly multilingual operator; its bike tours include night and beer tours and an Albufera trip with lunch and a lake boat trip.

Ceramics Workshop (Calle Rodrigo de Pertegás 42) Pottery classes with two of Valencia's top ceramicists, **Ana Illueca** (www.anaillueca.com) and **Susana Gutiérrez** (www.sweetsueceramica.com). Three-hour sessions (€65) from 4.30pm on Tuesdays. You'll make several pieces using different clays and techniques.

Valencia Bikes (☎650 621436; www.valenciabikes.com; Paseo de la Pechina 32; ⏰9.30am-8pm) Well-established bike-hire operation runs a daily three-hour city tour in English (€29.50/44.50 bike/e-bike).

Brisa (www.brisavalencia.es; Calle En Llopis 1) Has several city bike-tour options and an Albufera bike trip with lunch and a lake boat trip.

Guías Oficiales (www.guiasoficialescv.com) Accredited tour guides lead a two-hour €15 walking tour of the historic centre in English and Spanish starting from the City Hall tourist office.

Horta Viva (☎691 093721; www.hortaviva.net) Get to know the *huerta*, the market-garden area surrounding Valencia that provides wonderful fresh produce. Its Thursday paella cooking class is in English.

Poblados de la Mar (☎960 06 05 05; www.pobladosdelamar.com; walking tour €12) Informative Marga runs two-hour Thursday-afternoon walks in English around the El Cabanyal fishing *barrio*, with insights into architecture and traditional life (€20 per person; €120 per group if fewer than six).

Do You Bike (☎963 15 55 51; www.doyoubike.com; Calle de la Sangre 9; per day €9-15, per week €35-40; ⏰9.30am-2pm & 5-8.15pm) Daily city bike tour starting in Plaza del Ayuntamiento (€25 in English, more in other languages).

Responsible Travel

Valencia has over 2 million visitors a year. Tourism is key to its economy but can have a heavy environmental impact. The city is making great efforts to counter this with plans to become carbon-neutral in tourism by 2025 and carbon-neutral altogether by 2030. Everyone can help it lessen tourism's impact.

When & Where

Valencia has a great climate, so visiting in spring or autumn, or even winter, can be just as enjoyable as the summer peak...fewer crowds, easier reservations, more moderate temperatures, and culture and entertainment in full swing. Midweek visits often bring similar rewards compared with busy weekends.

Spending time and money away from the city centre – either in the outer *barrios* or by extending your trip into the interior of Valencia province – helps spread the tourism load, and the tourist euro.

Learn More

Read up on Valencia's ongoing sustainable tourism projects and responsible travel tips at visitvalencia.com/en/sustainable-tourism, visitvalencia.com/en/smart-tourism/intelligent-tourism and visitvalencia.com/en/smart-tourism/food-sustainability.

Go Local

Valencia has loads of independent shops dealing in everything from locally made fans, ceramics and hats to vintage clothing, vinyl and books. They're intriguing to explore and if you buy from them, rather than from chain stores, you'll be doing your bit for local small business.

When it comes to eating, you'll be eating local most of the time, as Valencia's *huerta* (market-garden area), the Albufera rice fields and the Mediterranean Sea supply most of what the city needs. If shopping for your own food, the municipal markets – including Mercado Central (p60) and others in El Cabanyal (p123), Russafa (p106) and the Barrio del Carmen (p75) are always stacked with fresh local produce and are fascinating places to browse.

Enjoy a guided tour to support local experts, from historians to architects.

MELINDA NAGY/SHUTTERSTOCK ©

Leave a Small Footprint

This is a great city for both walking and cycling, with a manageable scale, a lot of pedestrianisation, 160km of bike lanes and dozens of bike-hire outlets. It also has an excellent and cheap public transport system with a metro, trams, buses and suburban trains called *cercanías*. A car is more of a hindrance than a help, as parking and one-way systems can tie you up in knots.

Valencia has a very good fast-train service to/from Madrid, from where other fast trains fan out around Spain. No need to fly. There are good train links with Barcelona and Alicante too.

Climate Change & Travel

It's impossible to ignore the impact we have when travelling, and the importance of making changes where we can.

Lonely Planet urges all travellers to engage with their travel carbon footprint. There are many carbon calculators online that allow travellers to estimate the carbon emissions generated by their journey; try resurgence.org/resources/carbon-calculator.html. Many airlines and booking sites offer travellers the option of offsetting the impact of greenhouse gas emissions by contributing to climate-friendly initiatives around the world.

We continue to offset the carbon footprint of all Lonely Planet staff travel, while recognising this is a mitigation more than a solution.

Four Perfect Days

Day 1

V_E/SHUTTERSTOCK ©

Head first to the **Mercado Central** (p60; pictured) to experience it at its most bustling, then take your time to appreciate the Gothic charms of **La Lonja** (p62). Hit **Navarro** (p48) – having booked ahead before you reached Valencia! – for a rice lunch the way locals like it.

Next head to **La Catedral** (p56); check out the Holy Grail, then work off the carbs by climbing the bell tower. If you still have energy, visit the nearby ruins of **L'Almoina** (p67).

For dinner and drinks, it's definitely Russafa's enticing tapas zone. Get there early so you can browse some shops. Take your pick of the dozens of eating options that crowd these streets, then repair to **Cafe Berlin** (p99) for a cocktail.

Day 2

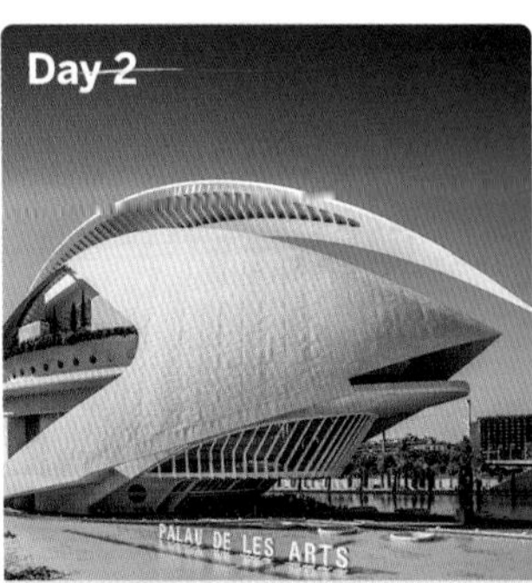

MILOSK50/SHUTTERSTOCK ©; ARCHITECT: SANTIAGO CALATRAVA

Head to the exhilarating **Ciudad de las Artes y las Ciencias** (p86; pictured). You may want to spend all day down here. Otherwise walk back along the riverbed-turned-park **Jardín del Turia** (p115) and dive into L'Eixample for lunch at **Las Lunas** (p91).

Next, sip *horchata* at the lovely **Mercado de Colón** (p91) then browse the boutiques of L'Eixample towards the **Estación del Norte** (p47), another Modernista marvel.

An evening in the Barrio del Carmen beckons. Stop at **Café Museu** (p81) to feel the bohemian local vibe. Dine on scrumptious tapas at **El Tap** (p79) or creative fusion at **Refugio** (p79), then hit **Jimmy Glass** (p82) for some top-class jazz.

Day 3

LUNAMARINA/SHUTTERSTOCK ©

Take in grand views from the **Torres de Serranos** (p77; pictured) before enjoying the **Museo Nacional de Cerámica** (p42) and nearby **Museo del Patriarca** (p44).

Lunch at **Entrevins** (p68) then cross to the **Museo de Bellas Artes** (p110) and spend some time with the greats of Spanish painting.

From here, it's a short hop to Benimaclet, where you might want to spend the evening in its offbeat cafes. Otherwise try one of Valencia's gastronomic restaurants – **Ricard Camarena** (p116) or Quique Dacosta's **El Poblet** (p48). Fancy a lighter meal? The same chefs run fun tapas restaurants too – **Canalla Bistro** (p101) and **Vuelve Carolina** (p48), respectively.

Day 4

JOSE_XERACO86/SHUTTERSTOCK ©

Hire a bike and pedal out to the beach. Breakfast overlooking the sands at **La Más Bonita** (p126), then follow the promenade south to El Cabanyal. Explore the characterful narrow streets, stopping for a tapa at marvellous **Bodega Casa Montaña** (p123) – if it has opened – or **Casa Guillermo** (p127).

Now pedal south out of the city to La Albufera (pictured). Take a boat trip on the lagoon and a stroll in the dunes. Watch sunset at **Mirador El Pujol** (p141).

At night, make a foray out to the university area. Squeeze into **Tanto Monta** (p118), then dine Moroccan in friendly **Balansiya** (p116). Head to **La Salamandra** (p118) for a quiet drink, or investigate the boisterous student nightlife nearby.

Need to Know

For detailed information, see Survival Guide (p147)

Currency
Euro (€)

Language
Spanish, Valenciano

Visas
From late 2023, the UK, USA and other countries not requiring an EU visa will need pre-authorisation to enter Spain (www.etiasvisa.com). Some nationalities will need a Schengen visa.

Money
Credit and bank cards very widely accepted.

Mobile Phones
Roaming charges within the EU have been abolished. Some non-EU phone contracts have free EU roaming. Local SIM cards available from phone shops.

Time
Central European Time (UTC/GMT plus one hour)

Tipping
Not widespread.

Daily Budget

Budget: Less than €100

Dorm bed: €20–40

Double room in a budget hotel: €60–80

Lunchtime set menu: €10–18

Bus ticket: €1.50

Midrange: €100–200

Double room in a midrange hotel: €80–140

Dinner in a midrange restaurant: €30–60

Short taxi trip: €5–10

Top End: More than €200

Tasting menu in gastronomic restaurant: €50–185

Double room in an upmarket hotel: €150–300

Useful Websites

Lonely Planet (lonelyplanet.com) Destination information, guidebooks, stories, features, videos and more.

Visit Valencia (www.visitvalencia.com) Useful official tourism site.

Booking.com (www.booking.com) The most useful hotel booking site for Spain.

Renfe (www.renfe.com) Book Spanish trains.

AU (www.au-agenda.com) Useful free what's-on magazine.

Valencia Secreta (www.valenciasecreta.com) Lively Spanish-language site with what's on, what to see and do, where to eat...

Guía Hedonista (www.valenciaplaza.com/guiahedonista) All things Valencia food (in Spanish).

Arriving in Valencia

The airport is an easy cab ride or metro journey from the centre, while the principal train station is fairly central.

✈ Aeropuerto de Valencia (Manises)

Metro Metro lines 3 and 5 connect the airport with central Valencia.

Taxi A taxi into the city centre costs €25 to €30 (including a supplement for journeys originating at the airport). The return journey is around €15 to €20.

Estación Joaquín Sorolla

Bus A free shuttle bus runs the short distance to Estación del Norte, on the edge of the old town.

Taxi A taxi from here to destinations around the centre will cost €4 to €7.

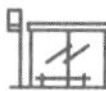

Getting Around

Central Valencia is very walkable, with much pedestrianisation.

Public Transport

The integrated bus, metro and tram network is efficient and useful.

Bicycle

An excellent network of bike lanes and the Turia riverbed park give fast, traffic-free access to large parts of town. Bike hire is widespread.

Taxi

Cheap and convenient, especially into the Ciutat Vella, where there is little public transport.

Car

Impractical for moving around the city, as well as being expensive to park.

Valencia Neighbourhoods

Barrio del Carmen (p75)
Historic old-town district that's just perfect for strolling, with a bohemian vibe and good restaurants and bars.

Western Valencia (p131)
An unusual zoo, a city museum and excellent parks and gardens are the highlights of this large area.

North Ciutat Vella (p55)
The heart of the old town is packed with character and must-see attractions.

Museo de Bellas Artes

La Catedra

La Lonja

Mercado Central

Museo Nacional de Cerámica y Artes Suntuarias

Museo de Patriarca

South Ciutat Vella (p41)
The busiest part of the old town, this is a civic centre with top shopping and worthwhile attractions.

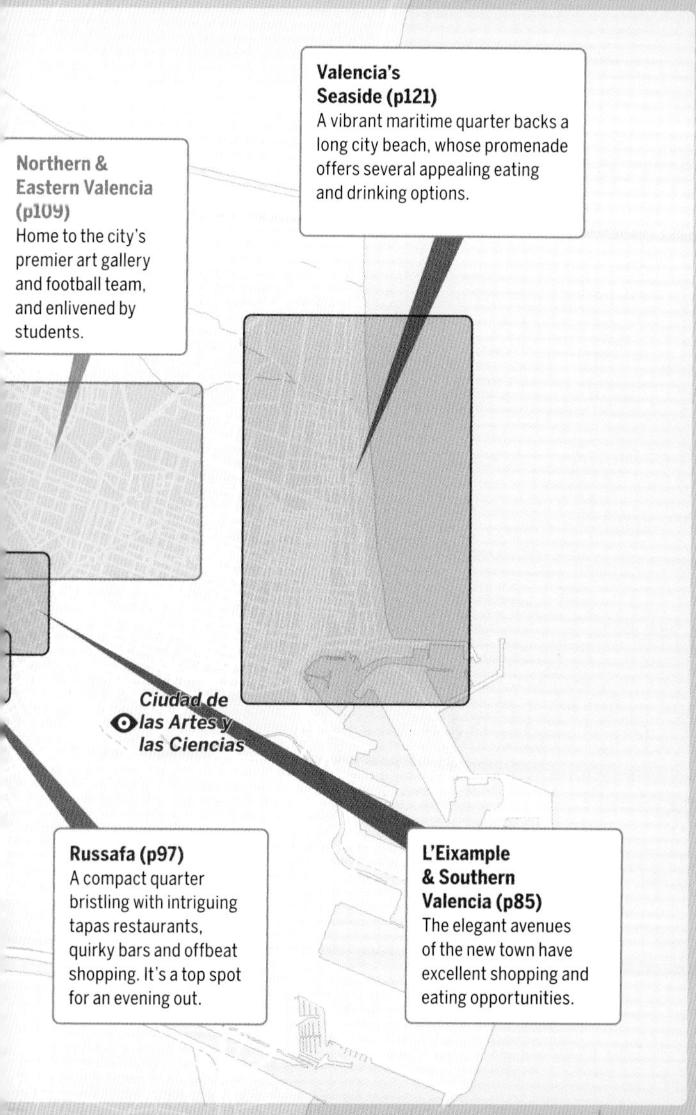

Valencia's Seaside (p121)
A vibrant maritime quarter backs a long city beach, whose promenade offers several appealing eating and drinking options.

Northern & Eastern Valencia (p109)
Home to the city's premier art gallery and football team, and enlivened by students.

Ciudad de las Artes y las Ciencias

Russafa (p97)
A compact quarter bristling with intriguing tapas restaurants, quirky bars and offbeat shopping. It's a top spot for an evening out.

L'Eixample & Southern Valencia (p85)
The elegant avenues of the new town have excellent shopping and eating opportunities.

Explore Valencia

Valencia's Walking Tours

Worth a Trip

Puente del Mar (p139) JOSE_XERACO86/SHUTTERSTOCK ©

Explore

South Ciutat Vella

The southern part of the old town, centred on the large city-hall square, Plaza del Ayuntamiento, is a busier, more commercial area than its northern counterpart. Valencia seems a big city here, with imposing buildings and metropolitan bustle. The shopping is first class, and there are several cultural attractions and plenty of accommodation.

The Short List

- ***Museo Nacional de Cerámica y Artes Suntuarias (p42)*** *Luxuriating in aristocratic splendour in a baroque palace which also holds a superb collection of Spanish ceramics.*
- ***Museo del Patriarca (p44)*** *Admiring works by El Greco and Ribera in a historic seminary-museum.*
- ***Navarro (p48)*** *Enjoying a perfectly prepared Valencian rice dish at this elegant, amiable restaurant.*
- ***Lladró (p50)*** *Picking your perfect porcelain at the famous Valencian ceramicists' boutique store.*
- ***Museo de la Seda (p47)*** *Learning about Valencian silk from caterpillars to velvet in a well-conceived modern museum.*

Getting There & Around

Bus: Plaza del Ayuntamiento and Avenida del Marqués de Sotelo to its south are a major bus hub.

M Xàtiva and Colón metro stations are on the edge of the zone.

Train: Estación del Norte is on the south edge of this area.

Neighbourhood Map on p46

Plaza del Ayuntamiento RRRAINBOW/SHUTTERSTOCK ©

Top Experience

Admire Superb Ceramics in a Sumptuous Palace

You get two exceptional experiences in one at Museo Nacional de Cerámica y Artes Suntuarias. It's set in the Palacio del Marqués de Dos Aguas, whose flamboyant decoration and furnishings make it arguably Spain's finest baroque-rococo palace. The top floor houses a first-class collection of Spanish ceramics, from medieval Islamic pieces to Picasso.

MAP P46, D1

www.culturaydeporte.gob.es/mnceramica

Portal & Carriages

The palace's alabaster entrance is as hyperbolically baroque as anything within. Two contorted figures symbolising rivers flank the doorway while the Virgin of the Rosary stands above. The portal was carved by Ignacio Vergara to designs of Hipólito Rovira, who was commissioned around 1740 by the third Marqués de Dos Aguas to transform a relatively modest mansion into a baroque palace proclaiming his aristocratic prestige.

The same Rovira-Vergara team created the splendiferous Carroza de las Ninfas, which is the star of the ground-floor carriage collection.

The Palace

The sixth marquis gave the palace interior much of its present character with a mid-19th-century makeover in mixed rococo, Empire and Chinese styles. On the 1st floor you pass from one sumptuously decorated room to another, with entirely antique furnishings and many original pieces from the palace itself. The aristocratic lifestyle climaxes in the splendid ballroom, but artisanry and detail throughout are superb. See paintings by Valencian Impressionist Ignacio Pinazo in the Pinazo room.

Ceramics

Valencia has long been a leading Spanish ceramics centre and the top-floor displays show how a fusion of Muslim and Christian artisanry yielded some of Valencia's most original earlier styles, notably the shiny lustreware which became a luxury item across 15th-century Europe. Other Valencian styles to admire include *socarrat* (unglazed but painted brick tiles, usually used for ceilings) and the colourful tile paintings which became popular in the 19th century. The exhibits finish with five pieces made by Picasso for the museum in 1955.

★ Top Tips

- Do scan the QR codes in the entrance patio to access the explanatory brochures (available in several languages), which will tell you what's what as you tour the palace.
- On the top floor, don't miss the fabulous painted and sculpted cupola in its own room off the first room. A creation of the versatile Rovira-Vergara team from the palace's 1740s revamp, it originally sat above the building's main stairwell.

✕ Take a Break

Federal (p48) is the perfect stop for a set-you-up breakfast before, or a light meal and drinks after, the visual feast of the museum.

For a fine meal in a slightly more formal setting, head nearby to Entrevins (p68).

Top Experience

See Fine Art in a Historic Seminary

The late 16th-century Seminario del Patriarca (Museo del Patriarca) was founded by San Juan de Ribera, a hugely powerful Counter-Reformation figure who wielded vast influence in Valencia, Spain and beyond. With an impressive Renaissance courtyard, its major appeal is a small but excellent religious-art museum. The archbishop-patriarch-saint endowed the seminary with a fine collection of what was then modern art.

MAP P46, E1

www.patriarcavalencia.es

Cloister & Chapel

The cloister-courtyard is a sober Renaissance space with two levels and columns of Carrara marble. In the centre is a later statue of the sainted anti-Protestant founder. The chapel on the right before you enter the courtyard, to which you'll usually be directed at the end of your visit, is dignified by tiles from Manises (a Valencian pottery centre) and Flemish tapestries.

Caravaggio

The roguish Italian master is represented in the museum by copies of two of his famous works, presumably done by students in his workshop. The *Judas Kiss* may have had substantial input from the master. One follower who learned the lessons of light and darkness particularly well was José de Ribera from nearby Xàtiva, whose chiaroscuro *Ecce Homo* here is very fine.

Thomas More

Remember *Wolf Hall,* where a doomed Sir Thomas More scribbled away in the Tower of London as he awaited his execution? It's a thrill to see here the very manuscript More was writing, visible inside a reliquary. A remarkable find, it was sent to Spain by More's daughter for safekeeping, and was rediscovered here in the 1960s. More didn't finish the work, as his papers and pens were confiscated.

El Greco & Juan de Juanes

El Greco is represented by a fabulous *Adoration of the Shepherds,* with the highly expressive faces so characteristic of his work, and by the Hamlet-like *St Francis and Friar León Meditating on Death*. Local boy Juan de Juanes was a deeply religious man whose biblical subjects, including two fine *Epiphanies* and a haunting *Nazarene* here, were beautifully realised.

★ Top Tips

- Though not part of the museum visit, it's worth going inside the seminary's fresco-covered main church (left-hand of the two street doors). Opening hours depend on Mass, usually once each morning and evening.
- In the church's vestibule you'll meet Lepanto, a hoary stuffed caiman. Though city legends say this was a monster that terrorised the Río Turia, it was actually a gift from the viceroy of Peru to his uncle Juan de Ribera, the seminary's founder. It became a much-loved pet of the stern Catholic, who had it preserved for posterity.

✗ Take a Break

Enjoy a fortifying dose of *cava* and freshly shucked oysters nearby at Ostras Pedrín (p49).

La Utielana (p49) provides no-frills, typical Valencian lunch options for a pittance.

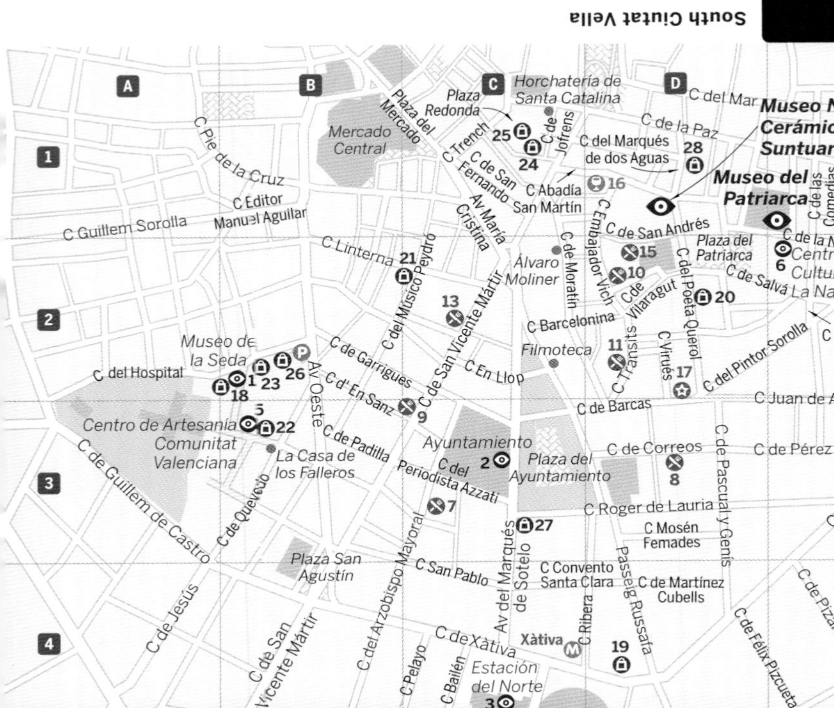

A
B
C
D
E
F
1
2
3
4
Museo Nacional de Cerámica y Artes Suntuarias
Museo del Patriarca
Horchatería de Santa Catalina
Plaza de Tetuán
Plaza Redonda
Plaza del Mercado
Mercado Central
C del Mar
C de la Paz
C de Jofrens
C del Marqués de dos Aguas
C Trench
C de San Fernando
C Abadía
San Martín
Luis Adelantado
C de las Comedias
C de Bonaire
C Pie de la Cruz
C Editor Manuel Aguilar
C Guillem Sorolla
Av María Cristina
C de San Andrés
C Embajador Vich
C de Moratín
Plaza del Patriarca
C de la Nave
Centro Cultural La Nau
Plaza Alfonso el Magnánimo
C Linterna
C del Músico Peydró
Álvaro Moliner
C de Salvá
C de Pintor Sorolla
C de Vilaragut
C del Poeta Querol
C del Poeta Quintana
C del Conde de Salvatierra
C de San Vicente Mártir
C Barcelonina
C Universidad
Museo de la Seda
C del Hospital
Filmoteca
C Transits
C Virués
C del Pintor Sorolla
C de Garrigues
C d' En Sanz
Av Oeste
C En Llop
C de Barcas
C Juan de Austria
Colón
C de Sorní
Centro de Artesanía Comunitat Valenciana
C de Padilla
Ayuntamiento
Plaza del Ayuntamiento
C de Correos
C de Pérez Bayer
Plaza de los Pinazos
C de Jorge Juan
La Casa de los Falleros
C del Periodista Azzati
C de Pascual y Genís
L'EIXAMPLE
C de Guillem de Castro
C de Quevedo
C Roger de Lauria
C de Colón
Mercado de Colón
C Mosén Femades
Plaza San Agustín
C del Arzobispo Mayoral
C San Pablo
Av del Marqués de Sotelo
C Convento Santa Clara
Passeig Russafa
C de Martínez Cubells
C de Pizarro
C de Jesús
C de San Vicente Mártir
C Pelayo
C Bailén
C de Xàtiva
Estación del Norte
Xàtiva
C Ribera
C de Félix Pizcueta
For reviews see
Top Experiences p43
Sights p47
Eating p48
Drinking p49
Entertainment p50
Shopping p50
0 200 m
0 0.1 miles

Sights

Museo de la Seda

MUSEUM

1 MAP P46, B2

The elegant Silk Museum is set in a Gothic-cum-baroque palace that in the 15th century was the seat of the Valencia silkworkers' guild. Silk was a major Valencian industry, and the exhibits take you through its history in Spain and Valencia, the lifecycle of the silk moth, and silk fashions through history. Upstairs has lovely restored rooms, the highlight being a fabulous rococo tiled floor depicting the fame of silk, here in woman's form, across four continents, represented by relevant beasts.

There is an excellent shop (p50). Pass through it into a recreated silk workshop with loom (active for group visits) and a pleasant patio with a restaurant. (www.museodelasedavalencia.com)

Ayuntamiento

MUSEUM

2 MAP P46, C3

Valencia's handsome neoclassical city hall dominates the plaza that takes its name. Explore the chandeliered grandeur of the function rooms and enjoy the view from the balcony. Within is the **Museo Histórico Municipal**, a repository of items important to the city's identity, such as the sword that Jaime I reputedly brandished when defeating its Muslim defenders, the flag they surrendered with, the Moorish keys to the city and a fascinating 1704 map of Valencia. (www.visitvalencia.com)

Estación del Norte

NOTABLE BUILDING

3 MAP P46, C4

Trains first chugged into this richly adorned Modernista terminal in 1917. Its main foyer is decorated with stained glass and mosaic 'bon voyage' wishes in major European languages. The wooden ticket booths are especially lovely. Don't miss the ceramic paintings by Gregorio Muñoz Dueñas in a room to your right as you enter.

Luis Adelantado

GALLERY

4 MAP P46, E1

This stylish spot is a local reference point for high-quality, current art exhibitions. It often has some real gems on display. (www.luisadelantado.com)

Centro de Artesanía Comunitat Valenciana

MUSEUM

5 MAP P46, B3

There is just one permanent collection room and one for temporary exhibits, but they show just how fine Valencian artisanry can be – beautiful traditional dresses, ceramics, silk, basketry, tiles, fans and more. (www.centroartesaniacv.com)

Centro Cultural La Nau

UNIVERSITY

6 MAP P46, E2

The base of the University of Valencia since its opening in 1500, La Nau has a harmonious cloister-courtyard lined with plaques of notable academics. Visit assorted exhibitions in the historic library and several other spaces. There's also a pleasant cafe. (www.uv.es)

Eating

Navarro
VALENCIAN €€

7 MAP P46, C3

A byword for its quality rice dishes (with other options too), Navarro has helpful service in an elegant green-toned interior and plenty of tables on the pedestrianised street. If you want a traditional Valencian paella (with chicken, rabbit, snails and green beans), or a vegetarian paella, you must ask one day ahead. Reservations advised. (www.restaurantenavarro.com)

El Poblet
GASTRONOMY €€€

8 MAP P46, D3

This upstairs restaurant, overseen by famed Quique Dacosta and with Luis Valls as chef, offers elegance and fine gastronomic dining strongly based on regional produce. It has sumptuous menus. Some of the imaginative presentation has to be seen to be believed, and staff are welcoming and helpful. (www.elpobletrestaurante.com)

Dulce de Leche
CAFE €€

9 MAP P46, C3

It's hard to walk past the displays of strawberry-covered cakes, quiches, croissants, cinnamon rolls and bursting *bocadillos* (filled rolls) at this buzzing cafe. Queue for breakfast to get great combos from eggs Benedict to açaí bowls. Later on it's calmer and a delightful haven for afternoon-tea lovers. (www.ddlboutique.com)

Federal
CAFE €€

10 MAP P46, D2

A bright international-style brunch-and-laptop cafe where you can eat pancakes with bananas, avocado toast, vegan burgers or bacon burgers and linger over a beetroot latte (or a straight americano). Later, there are salads, sandwiches, nasi goreng, pasta and a broad range of drinks. A pleasant, relaxed place to start or continue the day. (www.federalcafe.es)

Puerta del Mar
MEDITERRANEAN €€

11 MAP P46, D2

A good spot for a contemporary Mediterranean restaurant meal – plenty of rice options, seafood, meat dishes and salads, aubergines in tempura. It's well prepared without being radically pioneering, and served efficiently with a smile. The lunchtime set menu is a decent offering. (www.restaurantepuertadelmar.com)

Vuelve Carolina
MEDITERRANEAN €€

Overseen from a distance by noted chef Quique Dacosta, this upbeat bar-restaurant with decorative style offers inspiring tapas and fuller plates. These range from exquisite Peruvian- or Moroccan-influenced creations to tacos, rices, whole fish and more. It has crafty cocktails, too. Service is solicitous and you can sit at a table or the bar. (See 8 Map p46, D3) (www.vuelvecarolina.com)

Aladwaq

NORTH AFRICAN €

12 MAP P46,E2

Popular Aladwaq is the pick of a few North African restaurants in these narrow streets, and its vibe is inviting. The aromas alone might induce you to enter. It's delicious homestyle Moroccan fare, with a few eastern-Mediterranean-style dishes and good-value set menus. No alcohol is served. (www.aladwaq.es)

El Encuentro

SPANISH €€

13 MAP P46, C2

There's a likeable old-fashioned feel about this place, which offers stalwart Spanish cuisine at fair prices. Expect classics like Cantabrian anchovies, *pocha* beans with quail, and a variety of meat and fish plates. Space inside is limited but there's a pleasant summer terrace. (www.restauranteelencuentro.es)

Ostras Pedrín

SEAFOOD €€

14 MAP P46, E2

This pleasing little bar with white tiles, a backstreet vibe and a few tables in the back serves varieties of oysters, freshly shucked to order, and grilled or in tempura. They're great fresh, accompanied by a glass of *cava* (sparkling wine), white wine or vermouth. (www.ostraspedrin.es)

Horchata

A Valencian speciality, *horchata (orxata)* is an opaque sugary drink made from pressed *chufas* (tiger nuts; despite the name, it's a small tuber), into which you dip large finger-shaped buns called – no sniggering – *fartóns*. A traditional place to sample *horchata* in the heart of town is the colourfully tiled **Horchatería de Santa Catalina** (www.horchateriasantacatalina.com; Plaza de Santa Catalina 6). The Mercado de Colón (p94) has several choices too.

La Utielana

VALENCIAN €

15 MAP P46, D2

Tucked-away La Utielana merits a minute or two of sleuthing to track it down. Very Valencian, it packs in locals drawn by the wholesome fare and exceptional value for money. (www.lautielana.es)

Drinking

Café Madrid

COCKTAIL BAR

16 MAP P46, D1

Legendary birthplace of the potent cocktail *agua de Valencia* and once a celebrated bohemian-artistic hangout, Café Madrid has been revamped as an elegant (but not exclusive) cocktail bar with chandeliers and a fabulous offering of spirits and cocktails, many of the latter created or chosen by renowned Spanish mixologist

Cut-Price Cinema

A Valencia classic is the **Filmoteca** (http://ivc.gva.es/es/audiovisual; Plaza del Ayuntamiento), a cinema in the Teatro Rialto building that screens classic and art-house films in their original languages for a pittance (€2.50). It's so cheap some people might have just paid for a comfy place to snooze.

Esther Medina Cuesta. Try her Gin est Belle. (www.myrhotels.com/restauracion/cafe-madrid)

Entertainment

Teatro Principal

THEATRE

17 MAP P46, D2

One of Valencia's main performing-arts venues, with a fine 19th-century auditorium. It offers a varied program mostly of theatre, dance and opera, from September to June. (http://ivc.gva.es)

Shopping

Seda

TEXTILES

18 MAP P46, A2

At the attractive shop of the Museo de la Seda (p47) up one or more of the beautiful feather-light locally crafted silk scarves or shawls, or a tie, bag or fan. (www.museodelasedavalencia.com)

Sombreros Albero

HATS

19 MAP P46, D4

For all your hat needs, head to this venerable, thriving shop, run by the Albero family since 1820. There's an impressive range of berets, trilbies, Panama hats, cowboy hats, caps and more, and many hats are made by the family. (www.sombrerosalbero.es)

Lladró

CERAMICS

20 MAP P46, D2

More than 60 years ago, three Lladró brothers made the first of their famed porcelain sculptures. Today, their factory employs hundreds of people and exports figurines worldwide. Its Valencia retail outlet stands on one of the city's smartest streets. In what is almost a mini-museum, you can browse and purchase its winsome figurines. (www.lladro.com)

Cestería El Globo

ARTS & CRAFTS

21 MAP P46, C2

In business since 1856, charming El Globo has piles of traditional wickerwork – how about a basket for your bicycle? – plus walking sticks, hats and wooden toys. (www.facebook.com/cesteriaelglobo)

La Botiga de l'Artesanía

ARTS & CRAFTS

22 MAP P46, B3

The shop of the Centro de Artesanía Comunitat Valenciana (p47) presents a selection of fine contemporary Valencian craftwork

– original, often unique, handmade items from colourful silk shawls to jewellery, fans and tiles. (www.centroartesaniacv.com)

La Ruta de la Seda CLOTHING

23 MAP P46, B2

Find an original range of breezy clothing in lively printed fabrics. Mostly for women, the shop also does nice lines in shoes (including local Valencian espadrilles), fun beach bags and jewellery from around the world. (www.100pirata.com)

Las Ollas de Hierro ARTS & CRAFTS

24 MAP P46, C1

Valencia's oldest shop dates from 1793 and has an intriguing history and loads of character. Come November, its Las Fallas (p117) accessories and religious items are eclipsed by a wonderful range of figures and landscapes for Christmas Nativity scenes. (www.tiendadelasollasdehierro.com;)

Plaza Redonda ARTS & CRAFTS

25 MAP P46, C1

This circular 19th-century space in the heart of town – once the Mercado Central's abattoir – is ringed by stalls. Though it feels over-touristy after an elaborate makeover, there are some worthwhile shops selling traditional ceramics.

Librería Patagonia BOOKS

26 MAP P46, B2

Excellent travel bookshop with a great selection of maps and hiking-related books. (www.libreriapatagonia.com)

Valencia CF Tienda Oficial SPORTS & OUTDOORS

27 MAP P46, C3

A sizeable central shop offering shirts, souvenirs, scarves, woolly hats and mementos of the city's major football club. (www.valenciacf.com/es/stores/vcf/megastore)

Oxfam Intermón CLOTHING

28 MAP P46, D1

Oxfam's flagship shops in Spain are a long way from the charity-shop aesthetic. This is one of the best, with stylish clothing from sustainable materials and other fair-traded products and artworks. (www.oxfamintermon.org)

Dressing for the Party

Valencians take Las Fallas (p117) seriously. Find out how seriously at **La Casa de los Falleros** (www.lacasadelosfalleros.com), the place to buy traditional *fallera* dresses, men's jackets and breeches, or see roll upon roll of embroidered, sequined cloth and racks of off-the-peg dresses. A ready-made ensemble can cost well over €500, while made-to-measure starts well into four figures. Another central shop stocking Fallas materials is **Álvaro Moliner** (www.alvaromoliner.com).

Walking Tour

The Centro Histórico

This getting-your-bearings walk takes you past the historic quarter's major sights and monuments plus a selection of other intriguing buildings. It includes both the north and south of the old town, and a jaunt through the characterful Barrio del Carmen. Almost all along pedestrianised streets (but still watch out for taxis, cyclists and e-scooters), it could easily take a day or two if you explore all the sights.

Start Plaza del Ayuntamiento

Finish Plaza de la Reina

Length 2.7km; one hour

Numerous buses terminate in Plaza del Ayuntamiento.

Xàtiva is a short stroll from the walk start.

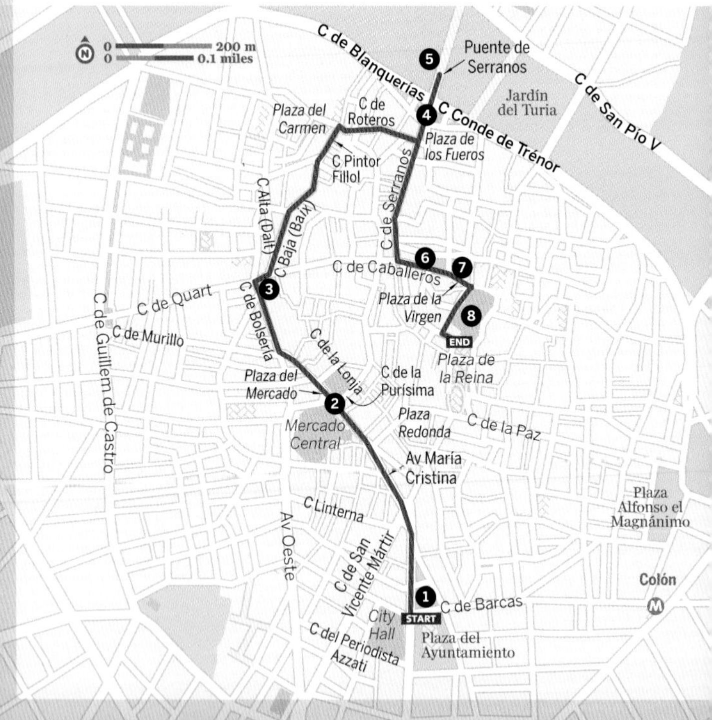

❶ Plaza del Ayuntamiento

Plaza del Ayuntamiento is flanked by noble civic buildings such as the **city hall** (p47) and a few incongruous American chain restaurants. It's Valencia's civic centre, a long, busy plaza narrowing towards the north – an arrow pointing into the heart of the medieval town.

❷ Mercado Central & La Lonja

Take the left fork from the plaza up Avenida María Cristina to Plaza del Mercado, where two of Valencia's finest buildings face each other. Glorious Modernista gem, the **Mercado Central** (p60) is the city's main market, while Gothic masterpiece **La Lonja** (p62) was once used by the city's merchants for trading goods.

❸ Plaza del Tossal

Continue up Calle de Bolsería to **Plaza del Tossal**. This landmark square is a meeting of many ways, one of which is Calle Baja (Carrer de Baix in *valenciano*), an important medieval thoroughfare that snakes its way into the heart of quirky Barrio del Carmen in the northwest of the old town.

❹ Torres de Serranos

Calle Baja becomes Calle Pintor Fillol and leads to Plaza del Carmen, overlooked by the church of the same name. From here, take Calle de Roteros – with its excellent tapas options – eastwards to the imposing **Torres de Serranos** (p77), once a major gateway in the city walls but now freestanding.

❺ Jardín del Turia

From the towers, cross onto the Puente de Serranos, a bridge leading to the city's northern region. It crosses a river that no longer exists: the Turia was diverted in the 1960s and its old watercourse is now a fabulous **park** (p115).

❻ Calle de Caballeros

Retrace your steps beneath the towers and head down characterful Calle de Serranos to Calle de Caballeros. The latter was medieval Valencia's main street and is lined with palaces and mansions, dominated by the **Palau de la Generalitat** (www.visitvalencia.com; Calle de Caballeros 2).

❼ Plaza de la Virgen

Emerge at **Plaza de la Virgen** (p67), a wide square with a famous fountain and a major city church. Valencians gather here in the evening and 'meet me by the fountain' is a standard beginning to a night out with friends.

❽ Catedral de Valencia

Head south until you reach **Plaza de la Reina** – recently liberated from traffic and attractively planted with trees. Here you'll see the entrance to the **cathedral** (p56) overlooked by the emblematic **Miguelete bell tower** (p59).

Explore

North Ciutat Vella

The heart of historic Valencia, this area contains several of the city's key sights and is many visitors' first port of call when exploring town. The cathedral's treasures include a chalice believed to be the Holy Grail, while the magnificent Lonja is one of the great Gothic civil buildings, and the handsome Modernista Mercado Central is one of Spain's most vibrant market halls. Other remnants of Valencia's storied past are scattered throughout the area, and there are plenty of good eating and drinking options as you explore.

The Short List

- ***La Lonja (p62)*** *Sensing the majesty of the principal hall at this sumptuous civil Gothic masterpiece.*
- ***Mercado Central (p60)*** *Working up a serious hunger while viewing the quality produce at this beautiful market hall.*
- ***Catedral de Valencia (p56)*** *Clapping your eyes on the supposed Holy Grail itself, and scaling the spiral stairs of the emblematic bell tower for unmatched views.*

Getting There & Around

Bus: Though most of the area is effectively pedestrianised, many buses, including 4, 8, 9, 11 and C1 (which does a loop round the Centro Histórico), pass through Plaza de la Reina in front of the cathedral.

M The closest stations are Alameda, in the Turia riverbed, and Pont de Fusta, just across it.

Neighbourhood Map on p66

Plaza Decimo Junio Bruto

Top Experience

Find the Holy Grail at La Catedral

The centrepiece of Valencia's old town, the cathedral is an intriguing place to visit, not least because it harbours nothing less than what's said to be the Holy Grail. It's a fairly low-slung building in truth, and impresses much more from within than without, though its soaring bell tower, El Miguelete, is a city icon.

MAP P66, D3

www.catedraldevalencia.es

Interior

Built over the city mosque (itself built over a Visigothic church) after the 13th-century reconquest, the cathedral's interior is low but spacious and atmospheric. The main structure is Gothic, while the side chapels with classical columns are mainly an 18th-century renovation. The nave's undecorated capitals and unadorned brick and stone give it an austere feel.

The Crossing

The most visually rewarding part of the cathedral, the crossing is topped by a picturesque octagonal tower instead of the more customary dome. The tower features two noteworthy tiers of arches with Gothic alabaster windows, built in the 14th and 15th centuries. On the half-dome above the altarpiece, vibrant Renaissance frescoes, rediscovered in 2004 under posterior baroque adornment, feature 12 musician angels acclaiming the Assumption, against a bright blue sky spangled with gold stars. By comparison, the baroque adornment of gilt cherubs, red marble and corkscrew columns seems like extravagant style over substance.

Don't miss the 14th-century Gothic pulpit, from which it is said San Vicente Ferrer, a famed Valencia-born preacher and missionary, preached in 1400. His portrait hangs above.

The altarpiece features beautifully restored Renaissance paintings of biblical scenes.

Transepts

The west transept boasts a fine Gothic rose window. The colourful 1960s stained glass in the east transept reimagines the seven 13th-century married couples carved in stone above the arch on the outside of this wall.

Museum

The cathedral **museum** (www.museocatedral valencia.com) is an attractive blend of the

★ Top Tips

- Most shops and several key sights in Valencia close for a few hours mid afternoon, but the cathedral stays open, making this a good time to visit.
- There's no charge to visit the cathedral from 7.30am to 10am (to 1.30pm Sundays), or from 6.30pm (5.30pm on Sundays) to 8.30pm, but this is when Mass takes place.
- El Miguelete is the only part of the cathedral open for tourist visits on Sundays from December to February.

✕ Take a Break

The restaurants immediately surrounding the cathedral are mostly mediocre tourist traps. Head to Delicat (p68) for exquisite tapas, or **Cappuccino** (www.cappuccinograndcafe.es; Plaza de la Reina 1) for a drink and snack beside the recently pedestrianised and tree-planted Plaza de la Reina.

modern and venerable. Its excellent religious paintings show the huge evolution in style in just one generation between the Renaissance paintings of Vicente Macip and those of his son, the great Juan de Juanes. The highlights, though, are the 10 wonderful 14th-century carved apostles, which used to flank the cathedral's west door. In the basement you can view Roman and medieval remains.

Capilla de San Francisco de Borja

Francisco de Borja, a 16th-century courtier to King Carlos I and empress Isabel of Portugal, had a rapid change of life after his wife died, entering the Jesuit order. The altar painting in this side chapel shows the event that launched his spiritual path. The two paintings that flank it are by Goya (1789) and show the duke bidding farewell to his family as he enters the holy life, and his intervention to save an unconfessed dying man, thwarting spooky lurking demons – prefiguring Goya's black paintings – in their nasty scheme to whisk the sinner downstairs.

Capilla del Santo Cáliz

This high star-vaulted chamber, built in the 14th century as a chapterhouse, apparently holds – suspension of disbelief alert – nothing less than the Holy Grail, a cup used by Jesus Christ at the Last Supper. It's viewed through the arch of a magnificent late Gothic alabaster screen, formerly the choir entrance. There are 12 Early Renaissance relief panels on the screen – the Old

El Miguelete, the cathedral's bell tower

Testament below, and the New above. The 'grail' itself is an agate vessel with medieval handles dating from about the 1st century CE, so at least the date is right.

Ambulatory

The 15th-century alabaster sculpture of the Virgin, *La Virgen del Coro,* is revered locally. Pregnant women walk nine times around the cathedral and pray to her for a successful delivery. Opposite, directly behind the altar, the Capilla de la Resurrección has a polished alabaster portico and the spooky left arm of San Vicente Mártir (tortured to death in Valencia in 304 CE), with ringed fingers and the odd hair still seemingly in place. Nearby, the Capilla de San Dionisio y Santa Margarita's fine late Gothic altarpiece is a work of Vicente Macip.

Other Chapels

In other chapels around the nave are six canvases of the life of Mary in the Capilla de San Pedro, painted by Nicolás Falcó (early 16th century), and Pedro de Orrente's impressive early 17th-century chiaroscuro San Sebastián in the chapel of the same name.

The Holy Grail

How did the Grail get here? The cathedral's version is that St Peter took it to Rome after the Last Supper. Passed down the line of early popes, it was sent to Huesca (Aragón, northern Spain) for safekeeping when Christians were being persecuted in Rome. After the 8th-century Muslim invasion it was hidden in the Pyrenees, winding up at the monastery of San Juan de la Peña. In 1399 the monastery gave it to the king of Aragón. It was kept at Zaragoza, then Barcelona, then, under King Alfonso V, at his palace in Valencia. In 1437 Alfonso gave it to the cathedral. its home ever since.

El Miguelete

Started in the 14th century, the cathedral's **bell tower** is a beloved city emblem. Its 207 chunky stairs spiral to unparalleled views of the historic centre. Interestingly, the perimeter and height are equal at 51m. Thirteen of its 14 ancient bells are still in use. The little one on the terrace strikes quarter, and half-hours; the big one, weighing 7.5 tonnes, strikes the hour. Think twice about being there at noon!

Top Experience

Sip Wine & Enjoy the Bustle of the Mercado Central

Valencia's central market is like market halls throughout Spain: row after row of well-stocked vegetable, seafood, meat and other stalls and the bustle and chatter of shoppers and stallholders. What's special are its grand scale and the sky-high quality and presentation of the produce – and the wonderfully bright, airy, early 20th-century iron-and-glass structure it's all housed in, the finest Modernista building in the city.

MAP P66, C4

www.mercadocentralvalencia.es

Seafood

For many, the most spectacular counters are in the seafood section. There are cephalopods aplenty, crustaceans galore and fish of all kinds – it's a good moment to bone up on some restaurant menu vocabulary. Anguiles El Galet is a classic stall that specialises in live eels.

Deli Stalls

An abundance of cured meats, cheeses, oils, wines and conserves projects an almost idealised version of Spain. Sliced small goods are vacuum-packed in a moment and their ultra-slim profile should satisfy carry-on requirements for even the most demanding of budget airlines. Solaz, near the southwest end, and Manglano, just inside the main (northeast) entrance, are among the best stocked.

Fruit & Vegetables

The pride of Valencia is its *huerta*, the market-garden area surrounding the city that produces crops galore on rich alluvial soil. A brief gaze at the plump tomatoes on display here invokes a notion of pure goodness.

Central Bar

A fine way to absorb the market ambience after a spell of browsing the aisles is to sit down with a glass of wine or cup of coffee in hand. The double-countered Central Bar is stylish and serves up very tasty tapas plates (€11 to €18, daily roll €6.50), though you'll probably need to queue. You'll find it near the southern corner.

Palanca

The undisputed monarch of the meat stalls, this centenarian butcher has some magnificent cuts on offer. Admire the premium sides of beef and *buey* (ox, but actually usually older cows) in the glass-paned freezer alongside.

★ Top Tips

- There's a helpful map of all the stalls just inside the southwest entrance.
- If you want something vacuum-packed, ask for *'envasado al vacío.'*
- Two quaint spired brick buildings flank the market's facade on Plaza del Mercado. The left-hand one is La Llotgeta, originally market administration offices. Today it's a cultural centre staging some interesting photography exhibitions.

✕ Take a Break

Several market stalls sell slices of cake or omelette and other bites to eat there or take away. The place to grab a pew, a wine and a tapa while watching the action is Central Bar.

For speciality coffee, head to the Retrogusto stall.

Just opposite the market's main entrance, Boatella (p69) is a classic stop for a drink and seafood tapas.

Top Experience

Leave Your Sins Behind as You Enter La Lonja

This splendid building, a Unesco World Heritage Site, was originally the city's silk and commodity exchange, built in the late 15th century when Valencia was booming. It's one of Spain's finest examples of a civil Gothic building, designed by architect Pere Compte, who was obviously at the peak of his powers. Two main buildings flank a citrus-studded courtyard.

MAP P66, C3

www.valencia.es/cas/cultura/inicio

Puerta de los Pecados

The 'door of sin' was meant to send a powerful message to merchants entering the Sala de Contratación about the dangers of sharp busines practice (we could do with a few more doorways like this today). The wide portal is decorated with tendrils and figures on both sides. They are worth a much closer look. some of the symbolism is obscure, but there are some very comical scenes. Look for slapstick battles with beasts, drunkenness, lust, an eagle nipping someone's undercarriage and two men seemingly masturbating (or defecating?) into bowls held by a woman, an image whose message is particularly obscure!

Sala de Contratación

Utterly magnificent, this imposing space has twisted columns ascending 17m to the star-vaulted ceiling and huge church-like Gothic windows with intricate tracery. It has the majesty of a cathedral, appropriately enough for a building that was intended as a cathedral of commerce. Here silk and wool were traded, and banking done, and the design was daringly modern for its time. The Latin inscription around the upper part of the walls is motivational, stating that honest mercantile conduct is a sure path to heaven. Two sessions of the Spanish parliament were held here in October 1937, when Valencia was Spain's capital during the civil war. A lovely restored doorway, which you can't pass through, gives on to a spiral staircase leading up to the building's tower – where merchants who defaulted on their debts were imprisoned.

Consulado del Mar

The main building opposite the entrance was where a tribunal sat to discuss maritime mercantile issues. It's a solid three-storey structure crowned by battlement-like merlons

★ Top Tips

- Groups commonly visit but are whisked through very quickly, so it's worth waiting in the courtyard if you want to enjoy the key rooms in relative silence.
- There's very little printed information around the site, so the audio guide is a good investment. It also includes information on the building's exterior, which is well worth examining.

✕ Take a Break

If you're visiting in the late afternoon or any time after noon Thursday to Sunday, seek out nearby Tyris on Tap (p70) for a satisfying craft beer in contrastingly informal surroundings.

Just around the corner, La Sénia (p69) does all-day tapas with a market-based focus.

Plaza del Mercado: An Architect's Gaze

Plaza del Mercado (Plaça del Mercat in *valenciano*) was for centuries Valencia's nerve centre. It is a dialogue between three forms of monumental architecture. The first is 15th-century **La Lonja de los Mercaderes**, a unique example of civil Gothic and on the Unesco World Heritage List. The second is the **Iglesia de San Juan del Mercado** (Iglesia de los Santos Juanes) whose baroque facade (1702) has the peculiarity of a platform in front with a row of small shops underneath. The third is the **Mercado Central**, an outstanding work of European Modernisme, inaugurated in 1928. It's endowed with a powerful metal structure that generates interior light while its domes take centre stage on the roof.

By Carles Dolç, *Valencian architect and urban activist*

above a handsome top-floor loggia (not visitable). Between the merlons and the loggia windows, a frieze of kings and mythical figures continues round the building to the Plaza del Mercado facade. Below the windows are shields of Valencia.

Ground Floor

On the doorway leading into the Consulado del Mar's ground-floor tribunal chamber (pictured p62) from the Sala de Contratación, look right for a saucy relief of the Devil indecently assaulting an animal with a pair of bellows. He appears to get his come-uppance on the left side. The chamber is notable for a fine Renaissance ceiling and panels of Jaime I, San Vicente Ferrer and a guardian angel made using the local *socarrat* technique, involving the application of pigment to lime-coated dry brick. There's a 10-minute video with background.

Sala Dorada

The 1st floor of the Consulado del Mar building is accessed by a staircase from the Lonja's citrus-studded courtyard. Staying with the medieval-sin theme, look up to see what is probably La Lonja's most renowned sculpture – a gargoyle of a masturbating woman on the corner of the building above as you ascend.

The 1st-floor hall is known as the 'Golden Hall' for its chief feature: a noble *artesonado* (decorated wooden ceiling), brought here from the former town hall. It's a stunning gilded and coloured piece of work from the early 15th century, almost nail-free, with scenes of music and battle between the beams, prophets and mythical scenes on the upper supports, and humans, flora and fauna on the lower ones. A 10-minute video interprets many of the figures – with closer views than you can get with the naked eye.

For reviews see
Top Experiences p56
Sights p67
Eating p68
Drinking p70
Entertainment p70
Shopping p71
200 m
0.1 miles
A
B
C
D
E
F
1
2
3
4
Hotel Puerta Serranos
Torres de Serranos
C Conde de Trénor
Puente de la Trinidad
C de San Pío V
Jardín del Turia
Plaza de los Fueros
C Pintor Fillol
C de la Cruz
C de Don Borràs
C de Santo Tomás
C de Serranos
C del Muro de Santa Ana
C Franciscanos
C Samaniego
C Conde Almodóvar
C Navellos
Plaza Décimo Junio Bruto
C Boix
C Pintor López
C de los Trinitarios
C Alta (Dalt)
C Baja (Baix)
C Landerer
C de la Mare Vella
C de Calatrava
Iglesia de San Nicolás
C de Caballeros
C del Pintor Zariñena
Plaza de la Virgen
C de Almudín
Almudín
C Juristas
C del Reloj Viejo
Nuestra Señora de los Desamparados
L'Almoina
C Almirante
C de Aparisi y Guijarro
C del Gobernador Viejo
Plaza del Negrito
C Alvarez
C Valencians
Plaza del Tossal
C de Quart
Torres de Quart
C Cadirers
C de la Purísima
Plaza Nápoles y Sicilia
C de la Barcella
Catedral de Valencia
C de Correjería
C del Moro Zeit
C de Murillo
C de la Carda
C Taula de Canvis
C de las Danzas
C de Bolsería
C En Bou
C Tapinería
C de Cabillers
C de Avellanas
C Milagro
C del Trinquete de Caballeros
C de Guillem de Castro
C de Santa Teresa
La Lonja
C de la Lonja
C Ercilla
Plaza de la Reina
Plaza Lope de Vega
Iglesia de Santa Catalina
C de Valeriola
Iglesia de los Santos Juanes
Plaza de Juan de Villarrasa
C Carniceros
C Balmes
C Pie de la Cruz
Plaza del Mercado
Mercado Central
C Trench
C de los Derechos (Drets)
Plaza Redonda
C de San Vicente Mártir
C de San Fernando
C Av María Cristina
C de la Paz
C del Mar
C del Marqués de dos Aguas
C de las Comedias
C Conde de Montornés
Plaza de Tetuán
Fundación Bancaja
C del Mar
C de la Paz
1
2
3
4
5
6
7
8
9
10
11
12
13
14
15
16
17
18
19
20
21
22
23
24
25
26
27

Sights

Plaza de la Virgen SQUARE

1 MAP P66, D2

This busy square ringed by cafes, the cathedral and other imposing buildings, was once the forum of Roman Valencia. The reclining figure in its central fountain represents the Río Turia, while the eight maidens with their gushing pots symbolise the main canals flowing from it to irrigate the *huerta*, the extensive market-garden area surrounding the city.

L'Almoina ARCHAEOLOGICAL SITE

2 MAP P66, E2

Beneath the square just northeast of Valencia's cathedral, the archaeological remains of Roman, Visigothic and Islamic Valencia shimmer through a water-covered glass canopy. Downstairs is an impressively excavated, atmospheric mix of Roman baths, forum buildings and streets (still paved with huge stone slabs), plus part of a Visigothic church and bits of the Moorish *alcázar* (fortress). (www.valencia.es/cas/cultura)

Almudín HISTORIC BUILDING

3 MAP P66, E2

The Almudín was built between the 14th and 17th centuries as the centre for storage and distribution of wheat brought in from the countryside. Murals around the upper walls inside record grain deliveries in the 17th century. The lofty arched hall is now used for concerts and art exhibitions. (l'Almodí; www.valencia.es/cas/cultura)

The Ratpenat

If you want a 'respect' animal to stick on your coat of arms, you'd think you could do better than a bat. But there it is right on Valencia's heraldic shield, and the Ratpenat (*valenciano* for bat) is the symbol of the city. Though there are the usual spurious tales about its arrival on the shield, the most likely is that it gradually evolved from a *vibra*, a female dragon figure common in popular mythology and tradition in this part of the Mediterranean.

Iglesia de San Nicolás CHURCH

4 MAP P66, C2

Recently given a magnificent restoration, San Nicolás features a baroque riot of 2000 sq metres of brightly coloured 17th-century frescoes painted over the Gothic vaulting. The altarpiece is in similar style, with golden corkscrew columns framing the twin saints who share the church: San Nicolás saving boys from the pickling tub, and San Pedro Mártir with a cutlass in his head. (www.sannicolasvalencia.com)

Fundación Bancaja ARTS CENTRE

5 MAP P66, F4

High-quality art exhibitions, often featuring major international names, are the main offering at this bank-run cultural centre. (www.fundacionbancaja.es)

Iglesia de los Santos Juanes
CHURCH

6 MAP P66, C4

Heavily damaged when set ablaze during the Spanish Civil War, this locally important church next to the Mercado Central is being restored to its elaborate baroque splendour in gold, white and brown. The notable ceiling fresco is being put back in place using digital technology and an old photo. The entertaining audio guide, activated on your phone by a QR code, is narrated by an actor impersonating the church itself. (www.mentavalencia.com)

Nuestra Señora de los Desamparados
CHURCH

7 MAP P66, D2

There's serious modern Catholicism at work in the circular baroque space here, with priests giving almost-nonstop services to the faithful, and a payment kiosk for dedicated Masses. The focus: a highly venerated statue of the Virgin of the Abandoned, patron of Valencia. Due to her slightly inclined pose, she's affectionately nicknamed La Jorobadita (the Hunchback). (www.basilicadesamparados.org)

Eating

Entrevins
SPANISH €€€

8 MAP P66, E4

With a quiet, restrained elegance, this upstairs restaurant makes a lovely lunchtime retreat from the street bustle and is handy for several nearby sights. Ask for a window table to watch passers-by and enjoy the tasty food. The quality set menus are top value. (www.entrevins.es)

Delicat
TAPAS €€

9 MAP P66, D2

At this friendly intimate option, the open kitchen offers an unbeatable-value set menu of samplers for lunch and delicious tapas plates for dinner. The memorable food has a range of Asian and Moroccan influences. Book ahead as the small space fills fast.

Tasca Ángel
TAPAS €

10 MAP P66, C3

Tiny, no-frills Tasca Ángel has been in business for 75 years. It's famous for fishy tapas, in particular its fresh and delicious grilled sardines, with a hit of garlic and salt. Sit at the bar, order them with a cold beer or white wine and find inner peace. (www.facebook.com/victorarenasvergara)

La Salvaora
SPANISH €€

11 MAP P66, C2

Refined but not expensive, intimate La Salvaora is decorated with portraits of flamenco stars. The menu includes typical Spanish favourites – sirloin steak, bull's tail, croquettes – but preparations are adventurous, and there are surprises like an Albufera monkfish-and-mussels stew. Quality is exquisite: for this standard set menus are a steal. (www.lasalvaora.com)

Boatella

TAPAS €

12 MAP P66, C4

Boatella's terrace is a fine spot for tapas and a drink while eyeing bustling Plaza del Mercado. Fresh seafood is the main speciality, but also consider the fried artichokes or the *esgarraet*, a Valencian salad of red peppers, salted cod and garlic. It's always busy but the waitstaff do a great job. (www.boatellatapas.es)

El Patio de Pepa

TAPAS €

13 MAP P66, C3

This tiny tapas joint is cosy and cordial, with well-thought-out decor and delicious, freshly prepared small dishes from tacos and salads to *huevos rotos* (broken fried eggs). (www.elpatiodepepa.com)

Lienzo

GASTRONOMY €€€

14 MAP P66, F3

The modish, formal dining room sees wonderful things done with seafood in particular. Lienzo means 'canvas': contemporary Valencian art brightens the walls and there's an artistic flourish to the presentation. There's consistent quality across the various tasting menus and service is impeccable. (www.restaurantelienzo.com)

La Pilareta

TAPAS €

15 MAP P66, B3

Earthy and century-old, La Pilareta is great for hearty tapas and *clóchinas* (small, juicy local mussels), available May to August. The rest of the year it serves *mejillones* (regular mussels), altogether fatter if less tasty. It has atmosphere in spades. (www.barlapilareta.es)

Valencia from Above

Valencia is very flat, so for a panorama you have to ascend human-made rather than natural elevations.

Ateneo Mercantil (www.ateneo-valencia.es; Plaza del Ayuntamiento 18) The *terraza panorámica* of this members-only club, 50m above street level, is open to all for drinks and great views over Plaza del Ayuntamiento.

Hotel Puerta Serranos (www.myrhotels.com; Calle de las Blanquerías 4) The relaxed roof bar is open late for views of Torres de Serranos and beyond.

El Miguelete (p59) More than 200 steps to the terrace of the cathedral's bell tower, 51m above ground level.

Iglesia de Santa Catalina (www.valencia.es/cas/infociudad; Plaza de Santa Catalina) Climb 119 tower steps to study the cathedral and other landmarks from a distance.

Torres de Serranos (p77) The old city's northern gate; views over Turia park and the Barrio del Carmen.

Torres de Quart (p77) The mighty western gate.

La Sénia

TAPAS €€

16 MAP P66, C3

This casual option does a tasty line in flavoursome Mediterranean cuisine, with a short menu based on fresh produce and quality conserves. Try the tomatoes topped with bonito! (www.tabernalasenia.es)

Drinking

Café Negrito BAR

17 MAP P66, C2

A local legend, this cafe-bar on a little old town square has an intellectual, socially aware clientele and art exhibitions often focused on sustainable development. A top spot to while away an evening, indoors or out. (www.facebook.com/cafenegritovalencia)

Tyris on Tap MICROBREWERY

18 MAP P66, C3

This microbrewery outlet has 10 taps issuing tasty craft beers by the pint and half-pint. Enjoy it on one of our favourite central terraces out front. Book brewery tours online. (www.cervezatyris.com)

Café de las Horas BAR

19 MAP P66, D2

Offers high baroque, tapestries, all music genres, candelabras, bouquets of fresh flowers and a long list of exotic cocktails. It's an intriguing place to stop for breakfast, coffee, tea or a *copa* (mixed drink). (www.cafedelashoras.com)

Sant Jaume BAR, CAFE

20 MAP P66, B2

Tiny Sant Jaume, a former pharmacy, is a haunt for local characters and features a marble counter and ornate wooden ceiling. Stop for a coffee, beer or *agua de Valencia* (cava and orange-juice cocktail) anytime, with plenty of outdoor tables. (www.cafesantjaumevalencia.com)

Beat Brew Bar COFFEE

21 MAP P66, A3

A mecca for coffee enthusiasts, this friendly spot has 120 different organic, plant-based drinks. It also offers tastings and demos and workshops on the art of fine coffee – so popular that cafe and shop opening is limited to a few days a week. (www.beatbrewbar.com)

Entertainment

Radio City LIVE MUSIC

22 MAP P66, B3

This top old-town music venue in its fifth decade hosts regular live reggae, flamenco or other music, and DJs nightly. An animated, red-toned place with an eclectic crowd and two bars (music in rear). Wednesday reggae nights are fun. Entry charge some nights. (www.radiocityvalencia.es)

Espacio Inestable LIVE PERFORMANCE

23 MAP P66, E3

Edgy space with innovative dance, circus and drama of sometimes spectacular quality. It's a notable reference point of Valencia's alternative cultural scene. (www.espacioinestable.com)

The Local Tongue

Valencia has two official languages: Spanish (*español* or *castellano*) and *valenciano*. Almost everyone is at ease speaking Spanish and increasing numbers of Valencians, particularly younger ones, handle the local language comfortably too.

Though many locals don't like to see it as such, according to linguists the regional language is a form of Catalan, a language shared with Catalonia, Andorra and the Balearic Islands.

But language can be an emotive and often political issue. In Valencia there's a constant to-and-fro as councils of one political stripe replace Spanish street names with the *valenciano* equivalents, then their successors change them back. The result is a little chaotic: some streets have a different name at each end. While the difference between the two versions is often minimal, it can still confuse. Since the majority use Spanish, we've elected to stick with it in most cases. Occasionally we use *valenciano* where it's clearly dominant, or it's the official version as in names like Russafa (Ruzafa in Spanish). Be prepared and flexible as you navigate your way around town.

Shopping

Artesanía Yuste — CERAMICS

24 MAP P66, D3

This lovely shop, tucked away on a square off Calle Tapinería, has an excellent array of colourful ceramics, with some fine tiles made with the *socarrat* technique. It's run by a second-generation ceramicist, sometimes seen at work here.

Simple — ARTS & CRAFTS

25 MAP P66, E3

Simple has an appealing melange of quality artisanal goods made in Spain: cosmetics, candles, spices, preserves, pottery, blankets, baskets, espadrilles, hats… (www.simple.com.es)

Needles & Pins — VINTAGE

26 MAP P66, C3

A sweet, independent boutique specialising in vintage finds from the '40s to the '90s. It has beautiful summery dresses, printed shirts, '70s jeans, stylish blazers, floaty skirts and its own line of handmade designs. (www.needlesandpinsvintage.com)

Madame Bugalú — FASHION & ACCESSORIES

27 MAP P66, C3

Stylish and fairly pricey by Spanish standards, it offers original and striking women's clothing and accessories. Sibling store Bugalú at Calle de la Lonja 6 has original fashion for both men and women. (www.facebook.com/bugaluvalencia)

Walking Tour

Modernisme Meander

While Barcelona was the capital of the decorative, dramatic Modernista architectural style, the Spanish strand of art nouveau that flourished in the late 19th and early 20th centuries, Valencia wasn't too far behind. Numerous buildings in the city's central areas are stunning examples of Modernisme, while so many others wink at it, with an unexpected flourish enlivening otherwise sober lines.

Start/Finish Mercado Central

Length 3.25km; 1½ hours

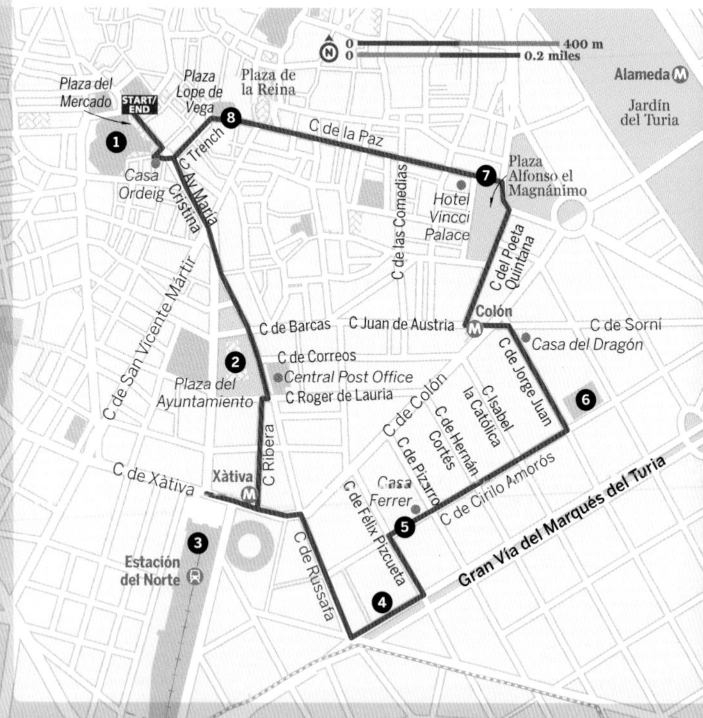

Casa Ordeig

art at the beautiful **Mercado** **entral** (p60), for many, Valen-a's greatest Modernista highlight. hen take in the elaborate stucco cade – with neo-Gothic pilasters bove allegories of Valencia's fertil- – of nearby **Casa Ordeig** on the rner of Calle Ramilletes.

Plaza del Ayuntamiento

llow Avenida María Cristina to **aza del Ayuntamiento**, flanked two splendid 1920s edifices at merit inspection despite being oclassical rather than Mod-nista: the **city hall** (p47) and the **ntral post office**.

Estación del Norte

the end of Calle Ribera, detour ghtly to the heartwarming **tación del Norte** (p47), with its timistic exterior, cute original odernista booking area of dark ood, and adjacent hall with aborate tilework.

Casa Ortega

ke Calle de Russafa, then turn t for **Casa Ortega** at Gran Vía with its ornate floral decoration d balcony, supported by a pair handsome caryatids.

Calle de Cirilo Amorós

left along Calle de Félix zcueta, then first right onto **Calle** **Cirilo Amorós**. Look above the modern, ground-floor shops to appreciate each building's original structure. Pause by **Casa Ferrer** (No 29), garlanded with stucco roses and ceramic tiling.

❻ Mercado de Colón

Continue northeast to the resplendent **Mercado de Colón** (p91), a chic spot for a drink surrounded by Modernista glory. Then head northwest on Calle de Jorge Juan, passing **Casa del Dragón**, named for its dragon motifs.

❼ Calle de la Paz

Head along Calle del Poeta Quintana to Plaza Alfonso el Magnánimo with its haughty mounted statue of King Jaime I, then left along **Calle de la Paz**. In the 19th century, Hotel Vincci Palace (Palace Hotel) was Valencia's finest. It and No 31, opposite, and No 36 (housing the Red Nest Hostel) sport elaborate, leafily decorated wrought-iron balconies.

❽ Back to the Market

On the corner of Calle de las Comedias, **No 21–23** has characteristically magnificent window-and-balcony work, and a columned top-floor mirador (corner balcony). Passing Plaza de la Reina, turn left off Plaza Lope de Vega into Calle Trench to return to the Mercado Central.

Explore

Barrio del Carmen

The northwest corner of the old town is the one that most retains an air of past eras, with its narrow medieval streets and still relatively bohemian character. El Carme, as it's known in valenciano, has some interesting museums and a great selection of little bars and restaurants to track down in its winding lanes. It's also fertile ground for Valencia's prolific street artists: you'll see some very eye-catching and thought-provoking works painted on a good number of walls here.

The Short List

- ***Torres de Quart (p77)*** *Climbing this mighty city gate for great views over the old town.*
- ***Institut Valencià d'Art Modern (p77)*** *Discovering the sculpture of Julio González, and other classy exhibits, in an airy contemporary gallery.*
- ***Jimmy Glass (p82)*** *Swaying to the rhythms at one of Spain's top jazz clubs.*
- ***Carmen dining (p79)*** *Enjoying some of the neighbourhood's small, characterful restaurants.*

Getting There & Around

The Carmen's narrow streets are definitely best accessed and explored on foot (or bicycle).

Buses stopping at the Torres de Serranos include C1 and 28, doing circuits of the Ciutat Vella, and 95 heading to the Ciudad de las Artes y las Ciencias and El Cabanyal.

Nonresidents' vehicles without a special permit are banned from almost the entire *barrio*. You can park in streets north of the Turia riverbed, a few minutes' walk away.

Neighbourhood Map on p76

Plaza de los Fueros, next to Torres de Serranos (p77)

For reviews see

Sights	p77
Eating	p79
Drinking	p81
Entertainment	p82
Shopping	p82

A
B
C
D
E
F
1
2
3
4
0 200 m
0 0.1 miles
Puente de las Artes
Puente de San Jose
C de Blanquerías
Jardín del Turia
Puente de Serranos
Pont de Fusta
C Conde de Trénor
Paseo de la Pechina
C de Liria
C de Salvador Giner
15
Centro del Carmen Cultura Contemporánea
8
C de Padre Huérfanos
5
C Na Jordana
23
C del Museo
2
Institut Valencià d'Art Modern
C Beneficencia
18
16
Plaza del Carmen
17
Museo del Corpus
Torres de Serranos
3
Plaza de los Fueros
C de Roteros
12
7
C Roda
C del Dr Chiarri
C Mirto
C Pintor Fillol
C Ripalda
Plaza del Árbol
C Franc scanos
C del Muro de Santa Ana
9
C de Santo Tomás
4
Museos de Prehistoria & Etnología
C de San Ramón
Plaza de Mossén Sorell
13
C de Corona
C Raga
C Baja (Baix)
11
C de Don Borrás
C de la Cruz
C de Serranos
C Samaniego
C Conde Almodóvar
C Navellos
C Alta (Dalt)
24
22
10
C Landerer
C de la Mare Vella
20
19
C de los Trinitarios
C de Guillem de Castro
C Dr Beltrán Bigorra
Plaza Vicente Iborra
Plaza del Músico López Chavarri
C del Pintor Zariñena
L'Iber
6
25
26
C de Caballeros
C de Almudín
Plaza de la Virgen
Plaza Décimo Junio Bruto
21
14
Plaza del Tossal
C de Pinzón
C de Quart
C Alvarez
C de Calatrava
C Cocinas
C Juristas
C del Moro Zeit
C de Bolsería
C Valencians
C Cadirers
1
Torres de Quart

Sights

Torres de Quart

GATE

1 MAP P76, A4

Spain's most magnificent city gate is quite a sight from its outer side. You can clamber to the top of the 15th-century structure, which faces towards Madrid and the setting sun. Up high, notice the pockmarks caused by French cannonballs during the Napoleonic invasion. (www.valencia.es/cas/cultura)

Institut Valencià d'Art Modern

GALLERY

2 MAP P76, B2

This impressive gallery hosts excellent temporary exhibitions and owns a small but impressive collection of 20th-century Spanish art. The most reliably permanent exhibition is the Julio González collection. This Catalan sculptor (1876–1942) lived in Paris and produced exquisite work in iron that influenced later artists such as David Smith and Eduardo Chillida.

The González collection was a major reason for the gallery's creation and there are some great pieces here – the series of sensitive iron *Masques* is exquisite – and they are beautifully lit and displayed. Contrasting with some classical nudes and busts, his offbeat iron forms are very much of his time and are sometimes reminiscent of paintings by Picasso (with whom González collaborated). González' pieces prefigure, on a modest scale, more monumental works later in the 20th century. (IVAM; www.ivam.es)

Torres de Serranos

GATE

3 MAP P76, E2

Once the main exit to Barcelona and the north, the imposing 14th-century Torres de Serranos overlook the Puente de Serranos, which crosses what used to be the Río Turia. Climb to the top for a great overview of the Barrio del Carmen and the riverbed park. (www.valencia.es/cas/cultura)

Museos de Prehistoria & Etnología

MUSEUM

4 MAP P76, B3

The enormous Beneficència complex, once a convent, holds two large, interesting museums which are entered on a single ticket.

The **Museo de Prehistoria de Valencia** (www.museuprehistoria-valencia.es) is an archaeological museum with some excellent pieces and loads of interesting information, but pick and choose or you'll be overwhelmed by the rows of flint tools and potsherds. It's strongest on the Roman era and pre-Roman Iberian culture. The **Museo de Etnología** (http://letno.dival.es) presents a livelier display focusing on Valencian life since the industrial age began. It's divided into three sections: the city, the *huerta* (irrigated farmlands) and wetlands, and the dry lands and mountains.Info in the museums is mostly in English. The complex also hosts concerts and some interesting temporary exhibitions, and it has a courtyard cafe.

Centro del Carmen Cultura Contemporánea

CULTURAL CENTRE

5 MAP P76, C2

This centre occupies the handsome Gothic and Renaissance cloisters and rooms of the monastery formerly attached to the church on the landmark Plaza del Carmen. It's in a fairly severe Cistercian style and devoted to temporary exhibitions – there are often several at one time – and the centre is always worth a visit for a stroll around the cloisters alone. (www.consorcimuseus.gva.es)

L'Iber

MUSEUM

6 MAP P76, D4

With more than 95,000 pieces on display and over a million in total, L'Iber, set in a historic palace, claims to be the world's largest collection of toy soldiers. The huge 4.7m x 2.8m set piece of the Battle of Almansa (1707) in the War of the Spanish Succession has 9000 combatants. Other dioramas and cases teem with battalions and regiments from antiquity to modern times and even a little science fiction. (www.museoliber.org)

Plaza del Carmen

Eating

El Tap

VALENCIAN **€€**

7 MAP P76, E2

The Tap is one of the Barrio del Carmen's rich selection of small, characterful restaurants. It's welcoming and professional, and the delightful food is market-based and original. Dishes with local tomatoes are a standout, and there's a carefully chosen list of wines and boutique beers. Excellent value; reservations are a good idea. (www.facebook.com/restauranteeltapvalencia)

Restaurant Blanqueries

MEDITERRANEAN **€€**

8 MAP P76, D1

Blanqueries excels in classy market-based set menus with creative (but not overly so) preparations of quality ingredients at good prices. Set menus include three different starters and then meat and/or fish (or a rice dish at lunchtime) for the main. The dining room is bright and tasteful without being too formal, and service is welcoming and polished. (www.blanqueries.com)

Refugio

FUSION **€€**

9 MAP P76, C3

Named for the civil-war hideout opposite, and simply decorated in whitewashed brick offset by colourful art, Refugio preserves some of the Carmen *barrio's* former revolutionary spirit. Excellent, innovative Med-fusion cuisine is designed for sharing and always has a variety of vegetarian, fish and meat options. Warm and welcoming. (www.refugiorestaurante.com)

Valencia's Walls

Valencia's two imposing gate towers – the Torres de Quart and Torres de Serranos – are all that remain of the medieval walls that used to girdle the city. The walls' line is traced by Calles Guillem de Castro, Xàtiva, Colón and Justicia and the south bank of the Turia riverbed – a rough oval that defines the Ciutat Vella (Old City). The walls were demolished in the 1860s.

Mestizo

CAFE **€**

10 MAP P76, D3

A sweet little cafe on a quiet street with friendly staff, great for a relaxed brunch, or a drink and tapa later. Mostly vegetarian fare, with Middle Eastern influences – much of it homemade. It does bowls of yoghurt with vegan granola and fruit, sourdough toasts with peanut butter and banana or labneh and spices, and ham-and-cheese croissants. Its speciality is coffee, organic and fair-trade. Plant-based milks available. (www.instagram.com/mestizovalencia)

Cantina Monterey

MEXICAN **€**

11 MAP P76, D3

Lively bar with a youngish, mostly local crowd, eclectic decor and genuine Mexican tacos made with maize tortillas by a Mexican cook. Select delicious flavours like *al pastor* (marinated pork), chipotle chicken, or cactus or pumpkin-flower for vegetarians. Sprinkle with coriander and chili-infused salsas, and accompany with tequila, a Modelo Especial or a *michelada*. This is Mex-Mex not Tex-Mex! (www.montereydiscos.es)

L'Aplec VALENCIAN €€

12 MAP P76, D2

L'Aplec prepares Valencian favourites, and some incomer options, as tapas plates or main dishes. A good place to try cuttlefish, octopus or shellfish. You could equally go for stuffed aubergines/peppers/tomatoes, fish, steak, salad or (if ordered ahead) a rice dish. The cooks know what they're doing and there's friendly service in a bright contemporary setting with thought-provoking art. (www.facebook.com/laplecvalencia)

L'Ostrería del Carme SEAFOOD €

13 MAP P76, C3

This stall inside the recently revamped Mercado de Mossén Sorell is a fabulous seafood snack stop. It has excellent-quality oysters from Valencia and elsewhere; sit down with a glass of white wine and let them shuck you a few. The petite, luminous market has a couple more tapas options and deli stalls. (www.laostreriadelcarmen.com)

El Celler del Tossal SPANISH €€

14 MAP P76, C4

An elegant, intimate, two-level spot a cut above tourist-focused places nearby, El Celler does a delicious line in market-fresh dishes involving fish, duck, rice, oysters, poached eggs and more. Set menus are a good way to sample the cuisine. The wine list focuses on small producers. (www.elcellerdeltossal.es)

La Tastaolletes VEGETARIAN €

15 MAP P76, C1

Pleasantly informal, La Tastaolletes serves creative, wholesome vegan and vegetarian food with quality ingredients. There's an international range of Buddha bowls and wraps, and tempting desserts (indulge in the hazelnut brownie with vanilla ice cream). And outdoor seating for decent weather. (www.latastaolletes.es)

Yuso VALENCIAN €€

16 MAP P76, D2

In a strategic location with tables on Plaza del Carmen, popular Yuso does good-value set menus, including at nighttime. Lunch menus always include rice dishes or *fideuà* (seafood-paella-like dish with noodles instead of rice). The quality is solid rather than spectacular. (www.restaurantesyuso.com)

Almalibre Açaí House

VEGETARIAN €

17 MAP P76, D2

This busy cafe doesn't just serve bowls of the Brazilian super-fruit açaí (with the likes of granola, *paçoca*, other fruits and assorted seeds) but also vegan burgers and wraps, quesadillas, rice bowls and plenty of fruity and other drinks – everything healthy! (www.almalibreacaihouse.com)

Drinking

Café Museu

CAFE

18 MAP P76, C2

A real forum for bohemian souls in the Carmen district, Café Museu is a popular local gathering spot for knocking back a few beers, maybe with a simple tapa or two. You can come for breakfast or *almuerzo* (Valencian second breakfast) too, and paella for €7.50 at Sunday lunchtime. (www.instagram.com/cafe_museu)

Beers & Travels

PUB

19 MAP P76, F3

A perfect spot for craft-beer lovers, with dark wood furnishings, a long bar with 29 beers on tap including local Tyris Amor Amarga and some potent Belgian drops, and tables out front facing broad Plaza de Manises. (www.beersandtravelsbar.com)

L'Ermità

BAR

20 MAP P76, D3

L'Ermità is a top local option for a drink, with decent music, cultural

Seafood paella

events, a friendly crowd of regulars and cordial staff. The quirky interior is comfortably cosy but can overheat: the outside tables on a quiet backstreet are prime territory on a warm night. (www.facebook.com/lermitacafe)

Trapezzio GAY

21 MAP P76, C4

On a broad Barrio del Carmen square, this well-established, purple-lit cafe and bar has a very mixed, relaxed clientele and is a fixture in the local gay scene. It has a great terrace where you can kick back with a drink. (www.facebook.com/trapezzio)

Entertainment

Jimmy Glass JAZZ

22 MAP P76, C3

Atmospheric Jimmy Glass is what a jazz club should be: dim lighting, a busy bar, and some top Spanish and international musicians. It only opens gig nights, usually Thursday to Saturday. Reserve by email (see the website), otherwise you'll only get in if there's space. It also runs an autumn jazz festival and usually spring and summer jazz cycles. (www.jimmyglassjazz.net)

Shopping

Pángala FASHION & ACCESSORIES

23 MAP P76, C2

A lovely shop doing a great line in 'slow bags', made by hand in Valencia in a relaxed manner. You'll find all kinds of bags here: they're all unique and there's a 'vegan' line. Other offerings include purses, neck warmers and small storage baskets. (www.pangala.es)

Santo Spirito Vintage VINTAGE

24 MAP P76,C3

This smartly styled vintage spot is one of Valencia's best preloved-fashion boutiques. It has Hawaiian shirts, printed blouses, colourful dresses, branded T-shirts and all kinds of denim garments, as well as pieces from Santo Spirito's own design collection. (www.santospiritovintage.com)

@typical Valencia GIFTS & SOUVENIRS

25 MAP P76, D4

This little shop lives up to its name with colourful, out-of-the-ordinary gifts and souvenirs – T-shirts, cards, mugs, prints – at reasonable prices. (www.atypicalvalencia.com)

Luna Nera FASHION & ACCESSORIES

26 MAP P76, D4

An original and atmospheric store with colourful, original women's clothing and accessories from around the world. There are lots of fun prints and always some interesting new arrivals. Prices are reasonable. (www.facebook.com/lunaneravalencia)

Paella & Other Rice Dishes

There's something life-affirming about a proper paella, but there's more to this most Valencian of dishes than meets the eye.

Types of Rice Dish There's a whole world of rices in Valencia. Paella has all the liquid evaporated, *meloso* rices are juicy, and *caldoso* rices come with broth. Rices reflect the seasons, with winter and summer ingredients making their way into the dish depending on the month. Almost any ingredient can be used, including all types of vegetables, fish, seafood and meat.

Paellas are typical of the Valencian coast. Meat paellas normally have chicken and rabbit, with green beans and other vegetables in summer, or perhaps fava beans and artichokes in winter. Fish rices tend to be more liquid, with squid or cuttlefish supplying the flavour and prawns or *bogavante* (like small lobsters) for garnish. *Arroz del senyoret* is a type of seafood paella cooked in a fish stock. If you add prawns to a meat paella, it's a *paella mixta*. *Arroz negro* (black rice) is another typical coastal rice that's made with squid ink and fish stock. *Fideuà* is similar to paella, but made with fine pasta (quicker to cook) instead of rice and a fish stock. Popular seafood-based winter rices include a cauliflower and salt-cod paella.

Secrets of the Rice The base always includes short-grain rice, garlic, olive oil and saffron. The best rice is *bomba,* which opens accordion-like when cooked, allowing for maximum absorption while remaining firm. Paella should be cooked in a large shallow pan to enable maximum contact with flavour. And for the final touch of authenticity, the grains on the bottom (and only those) should form a crunchy, savoury crust known as the *socarrat*.

Tips on Ordering For Valencians, rice is exclusively a lunchtime dish, though a few places do prepare it at dinnertime for the tourist trade. Restaurants should take around 20 minutes or more to prepare a rice dish – beware if they don't. You'll need two people or more to order a rice dish à la carte, and some require you to order in advance (you can check menus online). On weekends, heading to the beach, into the *huerta* or to Albufera villages such as Pinedo or El Palmar to eat rice dishes is a local tradition, but Valencians also love to get together at someone's house and cook up a rice dish themselves.

Explore

L'Eixample & Southern Valencia

L'Eixample (El Ensanche), which means the 'expansion', and was developed in the 19th century once Valencia got too big for its old walled town. It's a well-heeled zone of elegant streets, upmarket shopping and a great restaurant scene. Further southeast are the otherworldly buildings of the fabulous Ciudad de las Artes y las Ciencias, one of Valencia's major highlights.

The Short List

- ***Ciudad de las Artes y las Ciencias (p86)*** *Gazing in admiration at this majestic assemblage of futuristic architecture.*
- ***Mercado de Colón (p91)*** *Drinking and dining at a beautifully revamped Modernista market.*
- ***Palau de les Arts Reina Sofía (p94)*** *Listening to a soaring aria in the mothership-has-landed surrounds of this futuristic concert hall.*
- ***L'Eixample eating (p91)*** *Enjoying a brilliantly varied dining scene, less frenetic than nearby Russafa.*

Getting There & Around

For the Ciudad de las Artes y las Ciencias, bus 35 runs from the Estación del Norte via L'Eixample and Russafa; bus 95 runs from the Torres de Serranos.

M Colón station is handiest for the shopping district.

Line 10 (part of the metro system) runs from Alacant station to Russafa station (on the southern edge of L'Eixample) and on to the Ciudad de las Artes y las Ciencias.

Neighbourhood Map on p90

Palau de las Arts Reina Sofia and the Museo de las Ciencias Príncipe Felipe (p87) HELENA GARCIA HUERTAS/SHUTTERSTOCK ©, ARCHITECT: SANTIAGO CALATRAVA

Top Experience

Spend a Day at the Ciudad de las Artes y las Ciencias

This aesthetically stunning complex occupies a massive 1.5km-long swath of the old Turia riverbed. Its extraordinary buildings are mostly the work of world-famous, locally born architect Santiago Calatrava. He's a controversial figure for some Valencians, who complain about the expense and some design issues. Nevertheless, it's awe-inspiring stuff, and pleasingly family-oriented.

MAP P90, B2

www.cac.es

Palau de les Arts Reina Sofía

Brooding over the riverbed like a giant beetle, its shell shimmering with translucent mosaic tiles (the cause of quite a few problems) this ultramodern **performing arts complex,** (www.esarts.com; Avenida del Professor López Piñero 1) has four large auditoriums and a softening level of plants poking out from an upper level of the ceramic exoskeleton. Unless you have tickets for a performance (p94), a guided tour is the only way to enter. One-hour tours run five times daily (three on Sunday) in Spanish and English: book via the website.

Hemisfèric

The unblinking, heavy-lidded eye of the **Hemisfèric** (ww.cac.es) is at once planetarium, IMAX cinema and laser show. Film sessions – on themes like dinosaurs, the natural world and space – are roughly hourly, and multilingual soundtracks are available. Book ahead in summer, as it has limited capacity and often fills up.

Rent kayaks, rowing boats and other contraptions for a paddle on the surrounding lake.

Museo de las Ciencias Príncipe Felipe

The brilliant **science museum** (www.cac.es), stretching like a giant whale skeleton, has a huge range of interactive material in changing exhibits, ranging from DNA to space travel to viruses to the science of music. Its themes have good detail, incorporating issues like the environment and nailing that elusive concept of learning for fun. Loads of hands-on exhibits entertain children of all ages – and adults too. All info is available in English.

★ Top Tips

- Buy tickets for the Museo de las Ciencias, Hemisfèric and Oceanogràfic at www.cac.es to save time queueing. Combined tickets for any two or all three bring significant discounts.
- Many hotels in Valencia offer weekend packages that include entry to attractions at the Ciudad de las Artes y las Ciencias.

✕ Take a Break

Mediocre catering outlets are dotted around the complex and a restaurant, Contrapunto, is in the Palau de les Arts. Several more restaurants are across the Turia gardens on Paseo Alameda, and along Avenida Instituto Obrero de Valencia to the west, including excellent seafood at fair prices at **Sólo del Mar** (www.solodelmar.com; Calle Poeta Josep Cervera i Grifol 12).

L'Umbracle

This elegant 320m-long portal to the complex contains the car park and offices. Atop it, under a feathery ribbed roof, is a Mediterranean-cum-tropical garden whose southern end becomes a glitzy late-night bar (p94) in summer.

CaixaForum

Poking upwards like a giant purple mussel, the building known as the Ágora has since 2022 housed **CaixaForum** (www.caixaforum.org), which stages interesting art and other exhibitions on diverse themes. The spectacular interior has a roof reminiscent of a whale's backbone and ribs.

Oceanogràfic

Spain's most famous **aquarium** (www.oceanografic.org; Calle de Eduardo Primo Yúfera) is in the southernmost section of the Ciudad de las Artes y las Ciencias. The impressive display is divided into zones for different habitats and species, reached overground or underground from the central hub. The sharks, complete with tunnel, are a favourite, while beautiful tanks present species from temperate, Mediterranean and tropical waters. Less happily, the aquarium also keeps captive dolphins and belugas – research suggests this is detrimental to their welfare.

It's not all underwater. An aviary has wetland birds, while the

The Ágora (right) and the Puente de l'Assut d'Or (left).

Calatrava – Saint or Sinner?

Santiago Calatrava, the world-famous Valencian architect responsible for most of the Ciudad de las Artes y las Ciencias, is a mercurial talent renowned especially for public projects such as bridges, stations, museums and stadiums – futuristic creations designed to be experienced by thousands of people every day.

You'll recognise his grand-scale structures immediately, his signature as distinctive and easily recognised as the Coca-Cola logo. Technologically, he pushes to the limits what can balance, counter, take and impart stress in concrete, iron and steel. For Valencia, Calatrava is as significant as Gaudí remains for Barcelona. The Catalan's use of *trencadí* (slivers of broken-tile mosaic) and his fluid forms based upon nature have been a major influence on his Valencian successor. Calatrava's soaring structures, all sinuous white curves with scarcely a right angle in sight, also relate to things organic: the vast blinking eye of the Hemisfèric or the filigree struts, like veins on a leaf, of the Umbracle. Most of the complex is Calatrava's design and it's an unforgettable testimony to his talent and vision. Be sure to drop beneath the Puente de la Exposición in the town centre to the Alameda metro station with its soaring struts and bold curves. Calatrava felt that making public spaces beautiful had been forgotten in a postwar Europe bent on rapid reconstruction of shattered cities and sought to change that. His works glorify numerous cities throughout Western Europe and the Americas.

So, Santiago is a local hero? Not quite. While he's loved by many for helping put Valencia on the global map, he has also been criticised for budget overruns and structural issues with some projects. The Palau de les Arts went €45 million over budget and had structural problems, the Ágora took years to complete, and road safety of the Assut d'Or bridge that spans the complex has been criticised. Many of his projects in other countries have also gone vastly over budget, and several were halted when funds dried up.

His structures look brilliant, though, and a few generations from now the cost will be forgotten...if they hold together.

ocean islands section has giant tortoises. There are penguins, seals and sea lions, too. Though the dolphin shows are a black mark, the aquarium makes an effort to present information about climate change and depletion of the marine ecosystem.

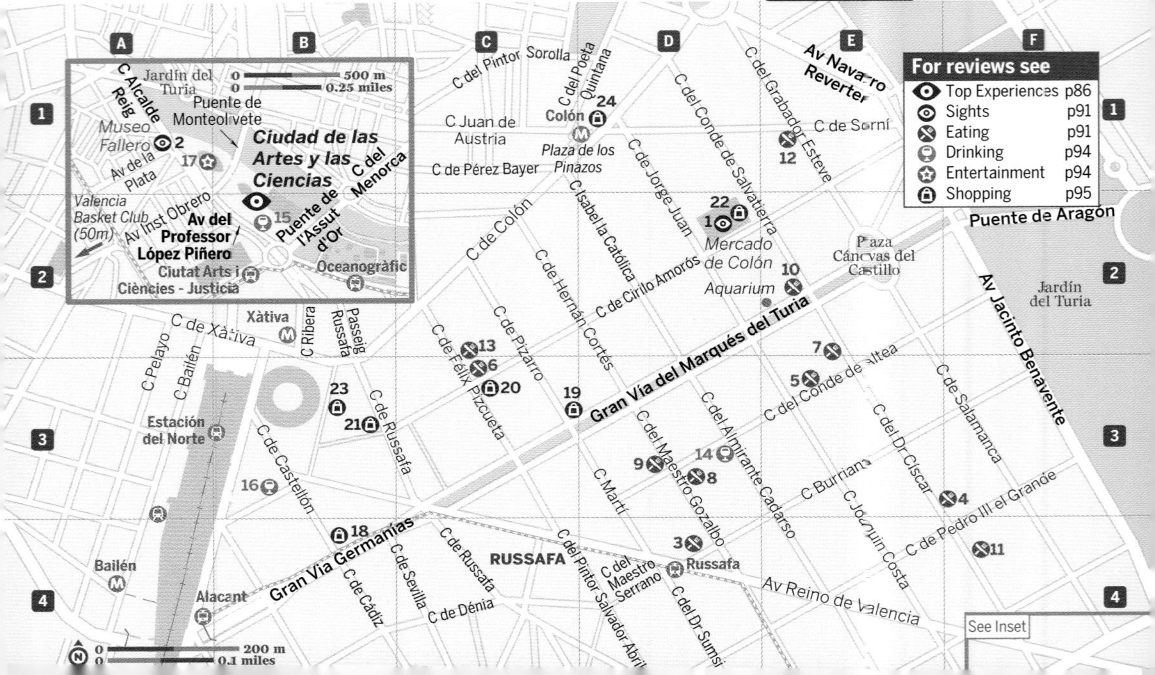

For reviews see

Top Experiences	p86
Sights	p91
Eating	p91
Drinking	p94
Entertainment	p94
Shopping	p95

A B C D E F
1 2 3 4

Jardín del Turia
C Alcalde Reig
Puente de Monteolivete
Museo Fallero 2
17
Av de la Plata
Ciudad de las Artes y las Ciencias
C del Menorca
Valencia Basket Club (50m)
Av Inst Obrero
Av del Professor López Piñero
15
Puente de l'Assut d'Or
Ciutat Arts i Ciències - Justicia
Oceanogràfic
0 500 m
0 0.25 miles
C del Pintor Sorolla
C del Poeta Quintana
24
Colón
C Juan de Austria
Plaza de los Pinazos
C de Pérez Bayer
C de Colón
C Isabel la Católica
C de Jorge Juan
C del Conde de Salvatierra
C del Grabador Esteve
12
Av Navarro Reverter
C de Sorní
22
1
Mercado de Colón
C de Cirilo Amorós
10
Aquarium
Plaza Cánovas del Castillo
Puente de Aragón
Jardín del Turia
Av Jacinto Benavente
C de Hernán Cortés
C de Pizarro
Xàtiva
C Ribera
Passeig Russafa
C de Xàtiva
C Pelayo
C Bailén
13
6
20
C de Félix Pizcueta
19
Gran Vía del Marqués del Turia
7
5
C del Conde de Altea
C de Salamanca
23
21
C de Russafa
Estación del Norte
C de Castellón
C del Almirante Cadarso
C del Dr Císcar
14
9
8
C del Maestro Gozalbo
C Martí
C Burriana
4
16
C Joaquín Costa
C de Pedro III el Grande
18
Gran Via Germanías
C de Russafa
RUSSAFA
C del Pintor Salvador Abril
C del Maestro Serrano
3
Russafa
11
Bailén
Alacant
C de Cádiz
C de Sevilla
C de Dénia
C del Dr Sumsi
Av Reino de Valencia
See Inset
0 200 m
0 0.1 miles

Sights

Mercado de Colón

MARKET

1 MAP P90, D2

The magnificent, airy Mercado de Colón, now colonised by cafes and boutique food outlets, was inaugurated in 1916 as a market to serve the rising bourgeoisie of the new L'Eixample suburb. Its handsome metal skeleton is garnished with Modernista flourishes to create a stunning ensemble. It's a good place to eat or drink (p94) and a fine refuge for families, as kids can run around and there's all-day food. (www.mercadocolon.es)

Museo Fallero

MUSEUM

2 MAP P90, A1

At each Las Fallas festival (p117), just one of the thousands of *ninots*, the figurines that pose around the base of each *falla* (huge sculptural ensembles of papier mâché, wood, polystyrene and other materials), is saved from the flames by popular vote. Those reprieved over the years are displayed here. It's fascinating to observe their evolution since the 1930s, and see the comical, grotesque, sometimes moving figures up close. Also on view are portraits of the *falleras mayores*, each year's 'queen of Las Fallas'. (www.visitvalencia.com

Eating

Goya

VALENCIAN €€

3 MAP P90, D4

Decorated with style and dedicated to guests' enjoyment, busy Goya blends traditional values and modern cooking. The menu has Valencian favourites such as delicious seafood rices and *fideuà*, but ranges widely with some avant-garde foodie bravura. Strong on presentation and great on taste. Reservations advised – at least a week ahead for weekends. (www.goyagalleryrestaurant.com)

Las Lunas

FUSION €€

4 MAP P90, F3

Unassuming but tastefully decorated and welcoming, Las Lunas has a brilliant-value lunchtime set menu of creative, succulent cuisine presented with flair. There are vegan choices. It also does an evening offer from Thursday to Saturday. (www.laslunassoulkitchen.com)

Fum de Llum

FUSION €€

5 MAP P90, E3

Small and informal Fum de Llum takes its food seriously and pleases everyone with creative Mediterranean fusion fare and amiable service. Offerings range from well-prepared rice dishes or *titaina* (a traditional Valencian tomatoes-and-tuna concoction) to duck-breast tataki or slow-cooked

A Classic on the Avenue

A legendary local stop for a morning coffee or a pre-lunch beer or vermouth, old-fashioned **Aquarium** (Gran Vía del Marqués del Turia 57) has a lived-in interior, wood panelling and white-coated waiters. Outdoor seating puts you in the buzz of the traffic and the flow of people. Indoors lets you scope out the cognac-and-cigar-gnarled local characters.

octopus or lamb. Set menus are a good way to savour the variety. Reservations advised. (www.fumdellum.com)

La Majada Quesos CHEESE €€

6 MAP P90, C3

Queso (cheese) lovers will adore this cheese-and-wine specialist restaurant and shop. It serves *tablas* (boards) of the best Spanish and some foreign cheeses in stylish, simple surroundings, with plenty of wines to accompany them. Complement the cheeses with salads, ham, burgers or croquettes. Reservations advised, especially on evenings when they have two sittings (8pm and 10pm). (www.lamajadaquesos.com)

Racó del Turia VALENCIAN €€€

7 MAP P90, E2

This intimate, traditional and classy spot with chandeliers and oil paintings is famous for well-prepared Valencian cuisine. Its rice dishes are a byword for excellence, among them the *arroz con bogavante* (rice with a kind of small lobster). Best to book, especially for weekend lunch. (www.racodelturia.com)

Ultramarinos Huerta TAPAS €€

8 MAP P90, D3

Occupying an old delicatessen-wine-shop with modern decor, Ultramarinos Huerta creates delicious innovative fare to enjoy among the attractive tiles, bottle shelves and deli counter. It's a good place to share dishes. Offerings include chicken cannelloni with Valencian cheese, *esgarraet* (Valencian peppers-and-salted-cod salad), omelettes and croquettes, or the 'bikini Comté', a buttery ham-and-French-cheese toastie! (www.ultramarinoshuerta.com)

Labarra TAPAS €€

9 MAP P90, D3

With a more local atmosphere than most places in the area, this large-ish tapas bar packs in customers for a standard range of tapas plates well prepared from quality ingredients – cured meats, cheeses, salads, ham and eggs, aubergines in honey, *escalivada* (smoky grilled vegies), breadcrumbed squid… It's an informal spot for a decent feed and drink at good prices. (www.facebook.com/labarramaestrogozalbo)

Baalbec

MIDDLE EASTERN **€€**

10 MAP P90, E2

Baalbec promises Mediterranean cuisine with the twist *'de la otra orilla'* (from the other shore) and makes good with tasty Moroccan/Middle Eastern fare in well-spaced surroundings with friendly service. Spanish ingredients are used in 'other shore' combinations – octopus with *babaganoush*, Iberian ham in vine leaves with tabouleh... Weekday lunch and dinner set menus are plentiful, though some might prefer spicier preparations. (www.baalbec.es)

Yarza

VALENCIAN **€€€**

11 MAP P90, F4

One of the district's classiest restaurants, with a semi-intimate atmosphere, Yarza has a strong suit in beautifully prepared seafood. Start with a plate of mussels and some *buñuelos de bacalao* (deep-fried balls of creamy cod paste) and continue with a rice dish (ordered in advance) or fish of the day. Service is super-professional, with quality reflected in the price. Reservations essential. (www.restauranteyarza.com)

La Petite Brioche

CAFE **€**

12 MAP P90, E2

A sweet little cafe with tempting croissants, cakes and quiches on a quietish street corner, La Petite Brioche is a pleasant spot for breakfast or a bakery snack any time. It also offers crêpes, fruit drinks and a good-value lunch menu of salad, quiche, dessert and coffee. (www.lapetitebrioche.es)

L'Encís

VALENCIAN **€€**

13 MAP P90, C2

A creative kitchen and enthusiastic, committed service characterise likeable L'Encís. The back dining room is a cool, pleasant spot to enjoy local ingredients in tasty, original preparations. Meats are cooked on an orange-wood brazier and even such humble cuts as chicken thigh are given quite a makeover. The weekday lunch menu is a good offer. (www.restaurantelencis.com)

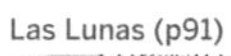

Las Lunas (p91)

Mercado de Colón

MEDITERRANEAN, ASIAN €€

Stop at this beautiful Modernista market building (See 1 Map p90, D2), now filled with restaurants and cafes, for a meal or drink without usually having to reserve. Downstairs, **Habitual** (www.habitual.es), an informal venture of Valencia celeb chef Ricard Camarena, has the best food. **Ma Khin Café** has good varied Asian fare. Or enjoy a leisurely *horchata* (typical Valencian sugary cold drink made from tiger nuts) or mojito. (www.mercadocolon.es)

Drinking

Angolo Divino

WINE BAR

14 MAP P90, D3

A cosy little bottle-lined bar on a typically lively L'Eixample intersection, Angolo Divino is a perfect spot to quaff a glass or two of quality Italian, Spanish or French wine. Plates of cheeses, ham and cured meats and focaccia make a great accompaniment. (www.facebook.com/angolodivinovalencia)

L'Umbracle Terraza

BAR, CLUB

15 MAP P90, B2

The open-air bar at the southern end of the Umbracle (p88) rooftop within the Ciudad de las Artes y las Ciencias is a touristy but atmospheric spot to spend a summer night, where you can catch the evening breeze under the stars. Downstairs club **Mya** is a sweatier experience. Admission covers both venues. You can prepurchase tickets online. (www.umbracleterraza.com)

Splendini

BAR

16 MAP P90, B3

An unusual but likeable little space that is both a secondhand-record shop – especially jazz but also soul, house, rock – and a cosy bar with wood-top tables where friends meet for a drink and relaxed chat with a jazz/soul soundtrack. Snacks such as pastrami *bocadillos* (filled rolls) and guacamole are available too. (www.facebook.com/splendinibaridiscos)

Entertainment

Palau de les Arts Reina Sofía

OPERA

17 MAP P90, A1

This spectacular arts venue, part of the Ciudad de las Artes y las Ciencias (p86), stages mostly opera and classical music, but also dance and flamenco and other genres. The main season is October to June.

Tickets cost from €10 to €145. Prices rise up to 20% once 70% capacity is sold, so it's worth booking ahead. There are discounts of up to 35% for ISIC (International Student Identity Card) and EYCA (European Youth Card) cardholders, retired people over 65, and last-minute tickets from two hours (one hour at weekends) before the curtain rises. (www.lesarts.com)

Shopping

Abanicos Carbonell ARTS & CRAFTS

18 MAP P90, B4

Historic fan-maker Carbonell, in business since 1810, offers hand-painted manual cooling units made from Valencian wood, ranging from a reasonable €10 for the basic but pretty ones, to works by famous fan painters that cost thousands of euros. It's been run by the same family for five generations. (www.abanicoscarbonell.com)

Linda Vuela a Rio PERFUME

19 MAP P90, C3

An elegant perfume shop specialising in boutique scents sourced from around the world. It's an enjoyably different experience, set apart from the supermodel-driven brands. The entrance on a corner of the elegant avenue is marked only by a painting of monkeys flanking Rio de Janeiro's Corcovado statue of Christ, above the doorway. (www.lindavuelaario.com)

Place CLOTHING

20 MAP P90, C3

With over 20 stallholders in one communal space, Place offers a bit of everything, from unique small-designer pieces to vintage clothing and creative accessories. (www.placevalencia.com)

Trufas Martínez CHOCOLATE

21 MAP P90, B3

The aromas are mouthwatering in this unassuming shop, where 80 years of experience have resulted in chocolate truffle perfection, as well as rich, dark handmade chocolates. The packaging is almost as delightful as the treasures within. (www.trufasmartinez.com)

Manglano FOOD & DRINKS

22 MAP P90, D2

Downstairs in the Mercado de Colón (p91), Manglano has brilliant cheeses, quality charcuterie and some wine. (www.facebook.com/charcuteriasmanglano)

Harmony Discos MUSIC

23 MAP P90, B3

Harmony has a great range of new and secondhand vinyl. It also stocks unusual rock-band T-shirts, both Spanish and international. (www.harmonydiscos.negocio.site)

Tenda Granota SPORTS & OUTDOORS

24 MAP P90, D1

It's sometimes easy to forget that Valencia has two football teams, so head here for a Barcelona-like replica shirt of perennial underdogs Levante. The shop's size, compared to Valencia's official shop (p51), emphasises the status gap between the teams. (www.tienda.levanteud.com)

LA PLACA
LA PLACA

Russafa

A downmarket barrio *turned trendy, Russafa (Spanish: Ruzafa) is comparatively compact but it packs a weighty punch. By day its collection of quirky galleries, arty cafes and vintage shops keeps people entertained. By night it becomes a buzzing hub of quality food and modish bars. Russafa has its own very distinctive feel and is an essential Valencian experience, particularly on weekend evenings when half the city seems to gather here.*

The Short List

- ***Dining (p101)*** *Hitting one of the multitude of quality restaurants and tapas joints, such as Canalla Bistro or El Rodamón de Russafa.*
- **Cafe culture (p104)** *Savouring the flavours of top-class speciality coffee with breakfast or brunch at cafes like Bluebell or Blackbird.*
- ***Vintage shopping (p107)*** *Searching for retro rags in Madame Mim and Russafa's other vintage-clothing shops.*
- ***Nightlife (p99)*** *Pounding the dance floor at clubs such as Piccadilly and Xtra Lrge.*

Getting There & Around

Buses through Russafa include the 35 between Plaza del Ayuntamiento and the Ciudad de las Artes y las Ciencias.

Russafa station is on tram line 10, part of the metro system, three stops from the Ciudad de las Artes y las Ciencias.

Russafa is in easy walking distance of the southern part of the old town.

Neighbourhood Map on p100

Apartments in Russafa DRG PHOTOGRAPHY/SHUTTERSTOCK ©

Walking Tour

A Night Out in Russafa

Russafa contains a staggering variety of eating options in a small area. Most lean towards modern, fusion cuisine, vegetarian fare or international specialities. It gets very busy at weekends, when the buzz is intoxicating and almost every intersection is surrounded by overflowing bars and restaurants. Tapas portions mean that you can go from bar to bar, trying different creations. It's the centrepiece of a great night out.

Start Cafe Berlin

Finish Piccadilly Downtown Club

Length 2km; time depends on you

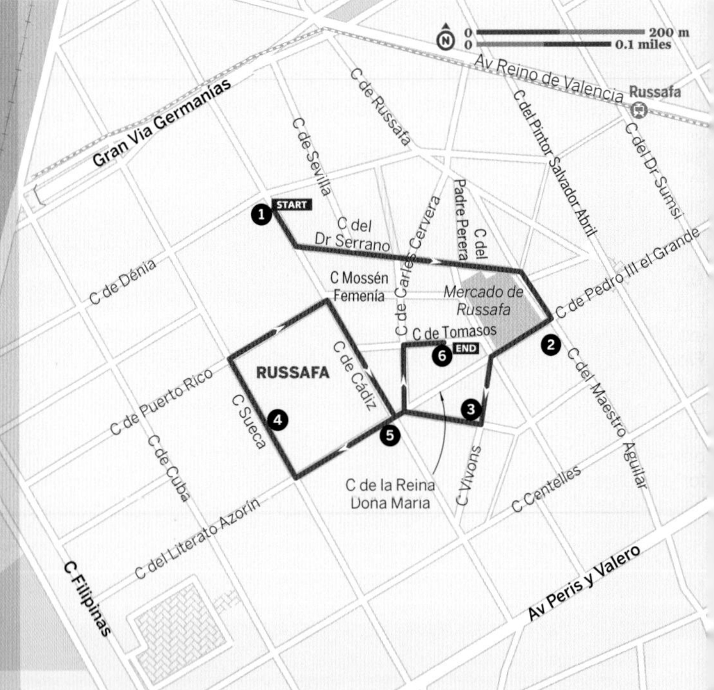

❶ Casual Beginnings

Start the evening at **Cafe Berlin** (www.facebook.com/cafeberlin valencia), one of many quality cafe-bars with a casual, arty, bohemian slant. It has a lounge-like ambience with books, art exhibitions, a whiff of incense and decent drinks, including well-made cocktails. It also does language-exchange sessions – a good way to meet locals.

❷ Modern Tapas

The eclectic range of small and medium dishes is delicious at **La Tasqueta del Mercat** (www.latasquetadelmercat.com), a bustling modern spot near the market. Order à la carte or through sampler menus. Some options are simply tasty, others are very good indeed: try the pesto/tomato/anchovy tapa and the brioche beef burger.

❸ Pizza & Beer

Likeably unrefined, the bustle extends out onto the street at **La Finestra** (www.facebook.com/la finestrapizzacafe), a popular backstreet place. The principal drawcard is its delicious mini-pizzas – staff choose the toppings for you. Beer is cheap too, so be happy if it's your round.

❹ Around the World

Excellent **El Rodamón de Russafa** (www.elrodamon.com) picked its favourite dishes encountered around the world and made tapas plates out of them. Choose from tacos, curry, Argentine-style steaks, temaki, ceviche and other eclectic dishes – plus a number of regular Valencian favourites. It's modern and buzzy, with professional and friendly service, great wines and high quality.

❺ Backstage Pass

Though it's been dolled up a bit since the old days, the **Backstage bar** on a key Russafa intersection is still a classic reference point. It's small, intimate and characterful: a great place for a post-dinner drink. True to its name, it preserves after-show ambience with coloured lighting, plastic-covered sofas and glory-days posters.

❻ Dance the Night Away

Round off the night at sizeable and fun **Piccadilly Downtown Club** (www.facebook.com/piccadillyvlc). Music focuses on major hits from the '80s and '90s, so there's no excuse not to dance. There's also a silent room, where you don headphones and choose from different sounds. Cover includes a drink; prebook at www.xceed.me.

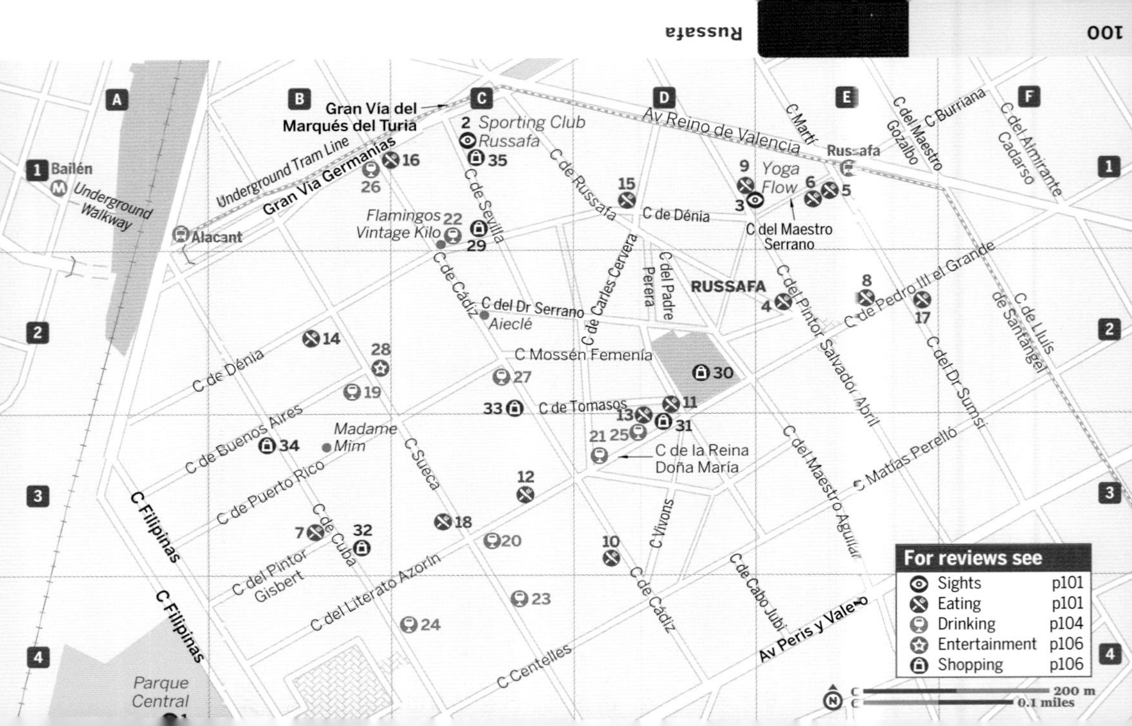
A
B
C
D
E
F
1
2
3
4
Gran Vía del Marqués del Turia
2 Sporting Club Russafa
35
Av Reino de Valencia
C Martí
Russafa
C del Maestro Gozalbo
C Burriana
C del Almirante Cadarso
Bailén
Underground Walkway
Underground Tram Line
Gran Via Germanias
16
26
C de Sevilla
C de Russafa
15
C de Dénia
9 Yoga Flow
3
6
5
C del Maestro Serrano
Alacant
Flamingos Vintage Kilo
22
29
C de Cádiz
C de Carles Cervera
C del Padre Perera
RUSSAFA
4
8
C de Pedro III el Grande
17
C de Lluís de Santàngel
C del Dr Serrano
Aieclé
C del Pintor Salvador Abril
C del Dr Sumsi
14
28
C Mossén Femenía
C de Dénia
27
30
19
33
C de Tomasos
11
13
31
21
25
C de la Reina Doña María
C de Buenos Aires
34
Madame Mim
C Sueca
C Matías Perelló
C del Maestro Aguilar
C de Puerto Rico
12
C Filipinas
7
C de Cuba
32
18
20
10
C Vivons
C de Cabo Jubi
C del Pintor Gisbert
C del Literato Azorín
23
C de Cádiz
24
Av Peris y Valero
C Filipinas
Parque Central
C Centelles
For reviews see
Sights p101
Eating p101
Drinking p104
Entertainment p106
Shopping p106
200 m
0.1 miles

Sights

Parque Central

PARK

1 MAP P100, A4

A long time in the works, this park is the first stage of what is conceived as a public space to join the two halves of Valencia that are still separated by the railway, which will eventually be put underground. Long-abandoned railway yards and workshops have been turned into a rare and pleasant modern example of a formal park, with lawns, ponds, trees and pathways lined by flowering plants. It has plenty of spots for kids to play. (www.valenciaparquecentral.es)

Sporting Club Russafa

ARTS CENTRE

2 MAP P100, C1

Once the HQ of a local football club, this offbeat space is run by a very active community-run arts organisation with the interesting subtitle Espai de les Arts contra les Arts (Space of the Arts against the Arts). Its exhibitions are often worth a look, and it hosts music, dance, drama, workshops, talks and other events. (www.sportingclubrussafa.com)

Yoga Flow

YOGA

3 MAP P100, D1

This modern yoga studio has classes in English or Spanish in two fresh and bright studios. You'll find everything from hatha flow for beginners to aerial yoga for the more advanced. Reservations are needed for some classes; prices drop for more than one class. (www.yogaflowvlc.com)

Eating

2 Estaciones

MEDITERRANEAN €€€

4 MAP P100, E2

Two talented chefs oversee this small, bright restaurant, where an open kitchen and welcoming folk provide a personal gourmet experience. Extraordinary creations are produced at reasonable prices (tasting menus €35 to €80); freshness and innovation are guaranteed. The seasonal menu can be tailored to dietary needs. There's pleasant outdoor seating. One of Russafa's best choices. (www.restaurante2estaciones.com)

Cervecería Maipi

TAPAS €€

5 MAP P100, E1

Far more traditional than most of trendy Russafa, the small tapas bar Maipi is a real delight. Delicious no-frills small and large dishes with excellent-quality fresh market ingredients. Prices are more than fair. (www.facebook.com/maipi.bar)

Canalla Bistro

FUSION €€

6 MAP P100, E1

Chic and animated, with quirky decor featuring, at last check, grotesque swine-head sculptures, Canalla is where top Valencian chef Ricard Camarena (p116) can be a little more lighthearted. Delicious and sensationally presented dishes draw their inspiration from street food around the world. Reservations strongly recommended. (www.canallabistro.com)

Dulce de Leche

CAFE €

7 MAP P100, B3

Delicious sweet and savoury snacks are the stock-in-trade of this delicately decorated corner cafe. The coffee is organic, the juices hit the spot, and the croissants, cakes, tarts and brioches are near-impossible to resist. The service is quality, but you might have to bring out your Mr Hyde to bag a street table. (www.ddlboutique.com)

Nozomi Sushi Bar

JAPANESE €€€

8 MAP P100, E2

Consistently rated one of, if not the, best of Valencia's numerous Japanese restaurants, Nozomi delivers one explosion of flavour and texture after another in its semi-minimalist dining room, where hundreds of paper birds float from the ceiling. The tasting menu shows off its range of preparations, from tempura to temaki, and includes eight delicious nigiri. Reservations essential. (www.nozomisushibar.es)

Mood Food

MEDITERRANEAN €€

9 MAP P100, D1

The harmonious interior of feel-good Mood Food is the scene for a limited but great menu of updated Spanish dishes with occasional oriental influences. It's a good spot for couples and you might share a couple of starters such as smoked eels or duck salad with kimchi before a main of steamed cod or two-month-matured beef. Service is amiable. (www.restaurantemood-food.com)

La Casa Viva

VEGETARIAN €€

10 MAP P100, D3

La Casa Viva is enticing for its cordial welcome and inventive, colourful vegetarian and vegan dishes presented with élan. Decor is cute, with low seats and plenty of greenery. (www.lacasaviva.com)

Osteria Vino e Cucina

ITALIAN €€

11 MAP P100, D2

Tiny Osteria (Italian for tavern) serves authentic Italian food with a smile. The handwritten menu has dishes made with ingredients from the Russafa market across the road, and the open kitchen serves perfect al dente pasta. A sister restaurant is a five-minute walk east along Calle de Pedro III el Grande. One or both of them opens every day. (ww.facebook.com/osteriavinoecucina)

Copenhagen

VEGETARIAN €€

12 MAP P100, C3

Bright and vibrant, the buzz from Copenhagen seems to spread a contagion of good cheer from its Nordic-style interior all along the street. It does toothsome plant-based burgers as well as top home-made pasta, but the truth is it's all pretty tasty. (www.restaurante copenhagen.es)

Blackbird

CAFE €

13 MAP P100, D3

A buzzy, popular breakfast spot with good-sized toasted sandwiches, homemade granola with seasonal fruit, and great cinnamon rolls. The Right Side speciality coffee is another draw. (www.facebook.com/blackbirdcafevalencia)

Café ArtySana

VEGETARIAN, CAFE €

14 MAP P100, B2

A welcoming, relaxed cafe in blue and wood that doubles as a creative space for local artists. The menu focuses on healthy food and local ingredients, mostly vegetarian or vegan. Choose from *bocadillos*, bagels, burgers, salads, fresh juices, smoothies and excellent homemade cakes. It has good-value brunch and lunch, Valencian craft beers and organic wines, too. It sometimes hosts events including live music.

Buñolería El Contraste

CAFE €

15 MAP P100, D1

Valencians have been coming to this corner cafe since the end of the 19th century to enjoy *buñuelos*. Made with pumpkin, this traditional Valencian snack is similar to a doughnut and particularly popular during the Las Fallas festival in March. Grab a bagful of deep-fried golden goodness and dip in sugar or hot chocolate for the sweetest of treats. (www.elcontraste.com)

Mood Food

Ultramarinos Agustín Rico

DELI €

16 MAP P100, B1

This spacious, bright deli and bar is hung with legs of *jamón* (ham) and lined with shelves of wine. Perch on a stool to enjoy, or order a *bocadillo* to take away and watch the owner stuff half a baguette with freshly sliced *jamón serrano* and cheese, drizzled with olive oil. (www.facebook.com/ultramarinosagustinrico)

Jardín Urbano

VEGAN

17 MAP P100, E2

The eclectic interior of this inviting corner cafe features books, a fountain, plants and artworks. Slightly removed from the hectic central Russafa scene, it also has a popular terrace out front and serves all sorts of plant-based eats from calzones and croissants to salads and avocado toast, and plenty of drinks, alcoholic and otherwise. (www.facebook.com/jardinurbanoruzafa)

Ultramarinos Agustín Rico

PENNY KIDD/LONELY PLANET ©

Gave Mx

MEXICAN €€

18 MAP P100, C3

Authentically tasty Mexican fare in cheerily colourful and informal Mexican surroundings makes for an enjoyable meal. A serve of four tacos or four enchiladas will set you back €10 to €12, and there's plenty more to choose from, including vegan options. (www.gavemx.com)

Drinking

Bluebell Coffee

CAFE

19 MAP P100, B2

Bluebell roasts its own super-quality coffee, sourced from female-led plantations and farms around the world. You might just come for the coffee. But the brick-arched space, full of animated chatter, also does excellent breakfasts – vegan granola, eggs Benedict, toast with poached egg and avocado. Quarter-kilogram bags of its coffee sell for €10 to €18. (www.bluebellcoffeeco.com)

Ubik Café

BAR, CAFE

20 MAP P100, C3

This bookshop-cafe with an old-fashioned feel is a relaxed place to lounge and browse. As well as shelves stacked with mostly secondhand volumes, it has well-selected wines by the glass, craft beers and good eats including vegan falafel, poke bowls, home-made pasta, ham platters and ecological burgers. It also stages art exhibitions and occasional live music, craft workshops and book presentations. (www.facebook.com/ubikcafe)

Mes Amours

WINE BAR

21 MAP P100, D3

Natural wines, grown organically, usually by small producers, and lacking the additives that go into conventional wine, are on the up. See what the buzz is about at Mes Amours, a tiny, neat corner bar with a few more tables outside. It has a long list of mostly Spanish varieties, and tasty homemade organic small plates to accompany. The wines might be orange (meaning the grape skins were not removed), pet-nat (light sparkling wines), glou-glou (for drinking young) or plain red/white/rosé. Bottles are mostly €25-plus but it also serves by the glass. (www.mesamours.es)

Slaughterhouse

BAR

22 MAP P100, C1

Once a butcher's shop (hence its title, also inspired by the Kurt Vonnegut novel of a similar name), Slaughterhouse abounds in books – new, old, for sale and simply for browsing. There's a selection of burgers, *bocadillos* and tapas to accompany your drinks in its relaxed artistic ambience. (www.facebook.com/slaughterhousefood-books)

Drinking the Local Water

Agua de Valencia is a popular local drink and refreshing indeed, but it couldn't be further from water. The usual recipe is to mix *cava* (sparkling wine), orange juice and a healthy dash of gin and/or vodka. It goes down a treat on a summer's day but packs a punch.

Planet Valencia

LESBIAN

23 MAP P100, C4

Right in the thick of things, Planet is the perfect after-tapas bar at weekends for girls looking for girls, but it's a fun place for anyone. (www.facebook.com/planetvalencia)

La Boba y el Gato Rancio

LGBTIQ+

24 MAP P100, C4

Run by welcoming folk, this relaxed gay cafe-bar, with arty decor and lighting, mixes a great cocktail and has a sociable little terrace out front. (www.facebook.com/labobayel-gatorancio)

Cuatro Monos

BAR

A cosy Italian-run bar with a welcoming vibe, Cuatro Monos

attracts regulars and travellers alike. The bar mixes monkey-inspired art with sofas, high bar tables and pavement seating. Try one of its special mojitos or a refreshing on-tap beer or local IPA.

Tapas and sandwiches are available and you'd do well to find a better *porchetta* (roast pork) sandwich outside Italy. (www.facebook.com/cuatromonosvalencia)

Xtra Lrge CLUB

26 MAP P100, B1

Spread over 600 sq metres, Xtra Lrge merits its outsized name. With a style of pastel colours against brute metal and concrete, it has live DJs in two distinct spaces, usually Thursday to Saturday nights. There's no cover charge and a pretty relaxed atmosphere. The crowd is more thirtysomethings than youngsters. (www.facebook.com/xlxtralrge)

Café Tocado BAR

27 MAP P100, C2

With the rich reds and romance of a French belle époque locale (and three pairs of sculpted Folies Bergère–style legs protruding from one wall), this place backs it up by actually having a small cabaret theatre alongside the intimate main bar. Top location on a central Russafa corner.

Entertainment

Café Mercedes Jazz JAZZ

28 MAP P100, B2

A super jazz club run by a real aficionado and with quality acoustics. There's usually live music on Friday and Saturday nights. A good after-dinner change of scene. (www.cafemercedes.es)

Shopping

Kowalski Bellas Artes ART

29 MAP P100, C1

A romantic treasure trove of a shop celebrating art – indeed the amiable owner is an artist and is often drawing or painting in the shop. He stocks an eclectic collection of quality new goods – artists' materials, books, vinyl, leather boots, trainers, shirts, jackets and more. A beautiful and curious place to browse. (www.facebook.com/kowalski.bellasartes)

Mercado de Russafa MARKET

30 MAP P100, D2

Forget Valencia's glorious Modernista markets for now. This concrete brutalist edifice plonked in the middle of Russafa, cheered up on the outside by coloured louvred friezes, is where it's at for good, fresh produce in this *barrio*, and the source of much of what you'll eat in local restaurants. Well worth a browse. (www.mercatderussafa.com)

Espanista

BOOKS, WINE

31 MAP P100, D3

A beguiling little shop, new in 2022, specialising in Valencian and other Spanish wines, craft beer and vermouth, plus an interesting range of books including Lonely Planet titles in English and Spanish. The amiable owner plans to make it a venue for exhibitions and Spanish classes. (www.theespanista.com)

Ultrasound

MUSIC

32 MAP P100, B3

A large store dealing in new and secondhand vinyl focused on the '80s, techno and EDM. It also has some T-shirts to go with its music.

Librería Bartleby

COMICS, BOOKS

33 MAP P100, C2

Bright and cheerful, Bartleby specialises in comic books, but also has an interesting selection of other books (everything's in Spanish). It also sells coffee and tea, and you can sip while browsing. (www.facebook.com/libreriabartleby)

Gnomo

GIFTS & SOUVENIRS

34 MAP P100, B3

Gnomo displays a limited but original and mostly inexpensive range of designer objects such as vases, lamps, bags and prints. The spacious layout is a design plus too. You might find a gift for somebody at home. (www.gnomo.eu)

Paranoid

CLOTHING

35 MAP P100, C1

Design your own T-shirt in this unusual shop, which also has preprinted tees. Its offbeat sideline is retro musical instruments. (www.facebook.com/paranoidtees)

Russafa Vintage Boutiques

Madame Mim (www.facebook.com/madame.mim.shop; Calle de Puerto Rico 30) Many Valencians would say this is the city's best vintage shop. As well as clothes, there's a line of quirky objects always worth a peep.

Aieclé (http://aieclevintage.es; Calle del Doctor Serrano 4) Celebrating all things vintage and reworked, Aieclé has rainbow-coloured shirts and blouses, upcycled sportswear, designer sweaters, denim and a raft of tempting accessories.

Flamingos Vintage Kilo (www.flamingosvintagekilo.com; Calle de Cádiz 17) Has mostly North American vintage clothing, which it sells by weight: jumpers, denim, leather jackets, colourfully printed dresses, Hawaiian shirts and more.

Explore

Northern & Eastern Valencia

This spread-out zone beyond the Turia riverbed is home to the two main universities, so well stocked with bars, restaurants and nightclubs. The Turia park, a 9km ribbon of greenery, is a strollable highlight. The city's main art gallery and Valencia football club are two pillars of local culture, while lively Benimaclet has alternative, community-driven happenings.

The Short List

- ***Jardín del Turia (p115)*** *Congratulating the citizen campaigners who got the riverbed converted into a glorious park and not a six-lane bypass.*
- ***Museo de Bellas Artes (p110)*** *Contemplating golden-age masters and local lad Joaquín Sorolla.*
- ***Valencia Club de Fútbol (p118)*** *Revelling in the atmosphere as the team tries to impress the nation's most demanding fans.*
- ***Benimaclet (p112)*** *Taking in the countercultural vibe of this traditional workers' neighbourhood.*
- ***Nightlife (p119)*** *Showing the night no mercy in top music venues such as Black Note and Matisse.*

Getting There & Around

M Aragó and Amistat stations are handy for the southern area. Tram lines 4 and 6, part of the metro, cross the northern part: pick them up at Pont de Fusta station, near the old town.

Areas near the Turia park are an easy walk from the old town.

Neighbourhood Map on p114

Puente de las Flores, Jardín del Turia (p115)

Top Experience

See Spanish Masters in the City's Top Gallery

The Museo de Bellas Artes, a somewhat unheralded spot across the Turia riverbed from the old town, boasts a truly impressive collection of local artists and Spanish masters. Housed in part of a former seminary, it's bright and spacious and ranks among Spain's best art museums.

MAP P114, B2

www.museobellasartes valencia.gva.es

Valencian Baroque

The museum starts with a long hall of Valencian Gothic and Renaissance religious art in glittering gilded settings. Then, El Greco's *St John the Baptist* is in room 6. Next up is 17th-century Valencian baroque art, which saw a new realism where Francisco Ribalta and his son Juan were important figures. Juan's *Preparativos para la crucifixión* is beautifully composed. Also influential was Pedro de Orrente: check out his pensive *Charlemagne*.

Velázquez

Head upstairs to the highlight room 15, for masters of Spain's 17th-century artistic golden age including Caravaggio-influenced local lad José de Ribera (from Xàtiva), Murillo, Alonso Cano... and Diego Velàzquez, who vies with Goya and Picasso for the title of Spain's greatest painter. His wonderfully penetrating *Autorretrato* (Self-portrait) here is a masterwork.

Goya

A handful of paintings against shadowy background by Spain's master of darkness are a high point of room 18. Though some may seem standard portraits, Goya's mastery of the unquiet behind the subjects' eyes marks him as a painterly force. Even the kids playing seem haunted by some impending doom.

Joaquín Sorolla

A two-floor wing (rooms 20 to 27) is devoted to this versatile Valencian artist (1863–1923), the leading light of Spanish art in the immediate pre-Picasso era. Sorolla at his best seems capable of capturing the whole spirit of an era through sensitive portraiture. *María convaleciente* is a stunning depiction of his daughter. The galleries also feature his forerunners, contemporaries and those he influenced.

★ Top Tips

- It's free, close to the old town, open until 8pm and doesn't close for lunch, so this is a flexible option when planning your agenda.
- Don't miss a stroll in the adjacent Jardines del Real.
- Find a floor plan in the Visita/Recursos section of the museum website.

Take a Break

The museum's pleasant indoor-outdoor cafe had been 'temporarily' closed for 2¼ years on our latest visit. If it hasn't reopened, you'll need to cross over to the old town for worthwhile eating options.

Consider continuing with the artistic theme by dining at **Lienzo** (p69). Its name means Canvas, and the food certainly is an art form.

Walking Tour

Cultural & Culinary Benimaclet

Once a separate community in the Valencian farmlands, Benimaclet, a short walk or metro or tram ride from the centre, conserves something of a village feel. It's an untouristic, fairly working-class neighbourhood, with a network of arty, socially aware and innovative bars and cafes that – as well as good food – produce a stream of cultural goings-on that mean there's something happening here almost every night.

Start Centro Instructivo Musical; **M** Benimaclet

Finish La Gramola

Length 2.2km; one hour

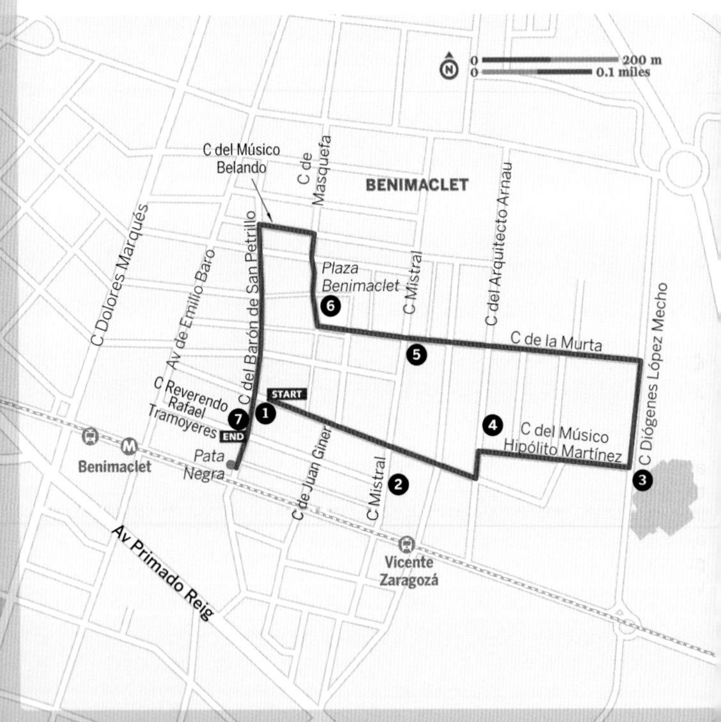

❶ Cultural Hub

Centenarian **Centro Instructivo Musical** (www.cimbenimaclet.com) doesn't look much with its big bare interior, but it's the soul of the *barrio*, and has been a generating force for a wave of cultural projects. Exhibitions, concerts, or beer and a game of pool: drop by and see what's on.

❷ Valencian People's Food

Head to **Ambra Poble-Bar** (p116) for a drink and snack. It specialises in *picaetes* (typical local tapas) and *coques* (Valencia's version of pizza).

❸ An Unusual Building

The '80s architectural project **Espai Vert** looks like the mother ship has landed on the edge of Benimaclet. A riot of quirky shapes, it was built as a cooperative aimed at developing a different way of communal living. The spacious apartments all have their own garden, whatever the level.

❹ A Literary Cafe

A slight trek north, **Kaf Café** (www.facebook.com/kafcafebenimaclet), hidden on a leafy plaza among apartment blocks, exemplifies the area's alternative vibe. At this literary cafe, reading is encouraged. It hosts exhibitions, music, poetry and debates. Food has a vegetarian/vegan emphasis.

❺ La Murta

A simple and informal all-day cafe, bar and **tapas stop** (www.facebook.com/barlamurta) in central Benimaclet. It has great-value tapas listed on the wall (in *valenciano*, but staff will probably speak English). Vegetarian options include melt-in-the-mouth crumbed rounds of goat's cheese.

❻ The Plaza

The peaceful little plaza, overlooked by the partly 16th-century church, breaks up the grid-like street plan. Grungy rock-bar **Glop** hasn't changed in years. The good-natured crowd spills onto the square in summer. From here, detour via Calle del Músico Belando, passing some old-fashioned townhouses.

❼ Dinner & Drinks

Appealing **Pata Negra** (www.patanegrarestoran.es) has flavourful dishes, and its leafy back patio and offbeat decor give it a curiosity-shop feel. Back up the street, **La Gramola** (www.lagramolabenimaclet.com; Calle del Barón de San Petrillo 9) mixes well-priced cocktails among plant-themed art.

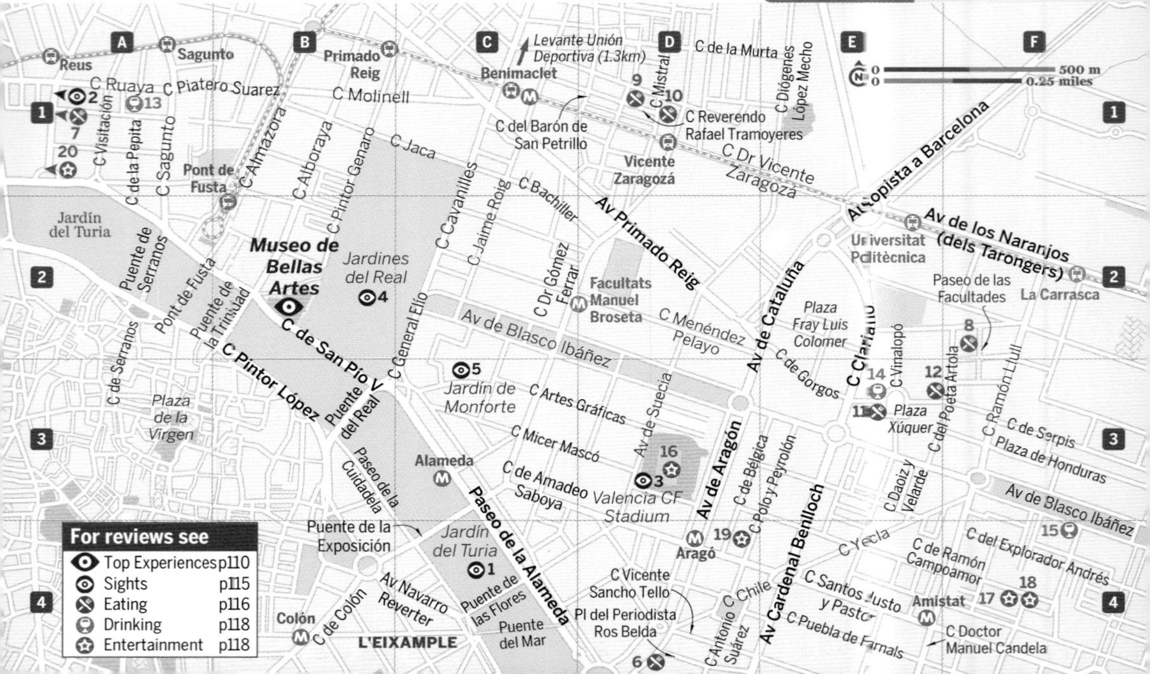

A B C D E F
1 2 3 4

Reus
Sagunto
Primado Reig
Benimaclet
Levante Unión Deportiva (1.3km)
C de la Murta
C Diógenes López Mecho
0 500 m
0 0.25 miles
C Ruaya
C Piatero Suarez
C Molinell
C del Barón de San Petrillo
C Mistral
C Reverendo Rafael Tramoyeres
Vicente Zaragozá
C Dr Vicente Zaragozá
Autopista a Barcelona
C Visitación
C de la Pepita
C Sagunto
Pont de Fusta
C Almazora
C Alboraya
C Pintor Genaro
C Jaca
C Cavanilles
C Jaime Roig
C Bachiller
Av Primado Reig
Av de los Naranjos (dels Tarongers)
Universitat Politècnica
Paseo de las Facultades
La Carrasca
Jardín del Turia
Puente de Serranos
Pont de Fusta
Puente de la Trinidad
Museo de Bellas Artes
Jardines del Real
C Dr Gómez Ferrar
Facultats Manuel Broseta
C Menéndez Pelayo
Av de Cataluña
Plaza Fray Luis Colomer
C Clariano
C Vinalopó
C del Poeta Artola
C Ramón Llull
C de Serranos
C de San Pío V
C Pintor López
C General Elío
Av de Blasco Ibáñez
C de Gorgos
Plaza Xúquer
C de Serpis
Plaza de Honduras
Plaza de la Virgen
Puente del Real
Jardín de Monforte
C Artes Gráficas
C Micer Mascó
Av de Suecia
Av de Aragón
C de Bélgica
C Polo y Peyrolón
C Daoiz y Velarde
Av de Blasco Ibáñez
Alameda
Paseo de la Cuidadela
C de Amadeo Saboya
Valencia CF Stadium
Paseo de la Alameda
Av Cardenal Benlloch
C Yecla
C de Ramón Campoamor
C del Explorador Andrés
Puente de la Exposición
Jardín del Turia
Aragó
C Vicente Sancho Tello
Pl del Periodista Ros Belda
C Chile
C Antonio Suárez
C Santos Justo y Pastor
C Puebla de Farnals
Amistat
C Doctor Manuel Candela
Colón
C de Colón
Av Navarro Reverter
Puente de las Flores
Puente del Mar
L'EIXAMPLE

2 7 13 20 9 10 4 5 8 12 14 11 16 3 19 15 18 17 1 6

For reviews see

Top Experiences p110
Sights p115
Eating p116
Drinking p118
Entertainment p118

Sights

Jardín del Turia

PARK

1 MAP P114, C4

Stretching almost the entire length of the Río Turia's former course, this 9km-long green lung is a fabulous mix of lawns, trees, playing fields, playgrounds and walking, cycling and jogging paths. It curves around the edge of the old city and onto the Ciudad de las Artes y las Ciencias, so it's also a pleasant way of getting around. See Lilliputian kids scrambling over a magnificent, ever-patient **Gulliver** (Jardín del Turia; 19, 95) south of the Palau de la Música concert hall. (www.jardindelturia.com)

Bombas Gens

GALLERY

2 MAP P114, A1

This art-deco factory that once made hydraulic pumps has been converted into an intriguing contemporary-art space. It normally has two or three thought-provoking temporary exhibitions in the appealing high-ceilinged spaces. The backyard has been turned into a garden of Mediterranean trees and flowering plants. The project, which receives no public funding, also has the restaurant (p116) of Valencian master-chef Ricard Camarena.

Join a guided tour on Saturday or Sunday to see the building's Civil War bomb shelter and medieval cellar. (www.bombasgens.com)

Jardín del Turia

Valencia CF Stadium

STADIUM

3 MAP P114, D3

A guided visit to Valencia's famous Mestalla stadium takes you to the press and trophy rooms, the changing rooms and out through the tunnel onto the hallowed turf. Hours change by season and according to fixtures: check the website. (www.valenciacf.com/en/tickets/forevertour)

Jardines del Real

PARK

4 MAP P114, B2

Stretching 700m north from the road flanking the Turia riverbed, these gardens are a lovely spot for a stroll, with plenty of palms and orange trees as well as a small aviary. Once the grounds of a royal palace, they're often called Los

Viveros (Nursery Gardens). (www.valencia.es)

Jardín de Monforte GARDENS

5 MAP P114, C3

The neoclassical-style ornamental Monforte gardens were created from a vegetable garden by Sebastián Monleón for the Marqués de San Juan in the mid-19th century. It's a peaceful break from the city bustle, with marble statues, sculpted hedges, a goldfish-speckled pond and walkways shaded by canopies of flowering vines – welcome relief from summer heat. The small but grand entrance pavilion and its picturesque backdrop make this a popular spot for weddings. (www.jardins.valencia.es)

Eating

Gran Azul VALENCIAN €€€

6 MAP P114, D4

Spacious and stylish, this main-road spot is a temple to excellent dining. It focuses on rice dishes and the grill, with premium-quality steaks and superb fresh fish simply done and garnished with flair. (www.granazulrestaurante.com)

Ricard Camarena GASTRONOMY €€€

7 MAP P114, A1

Valencia's highest-rated current chef showcases his abilities in the Bombas Gens (p115) factory turned art centre. Tasting menus (€185 plus drinks) focus on the Valencian ideal of fresh market produce, presented in imaginative combinations that bring out exceptional and subtle flavours. (www.ricardcamarenarestaurant.com)

Balansiya MOROCCAN €€

8 MAP P114, F2

This welcoming restaurant in a student neighbourhood near the university is elegantly decorated in Moroccan style. Its wide range of Moroccan dishes includes excellent sweets. The aromas will have you slavering. No alcohol, though there's a long list of nonalcoholic wines. Its homemade hibiscus drink is the way to go. (www.balansiya.com)

El Carabasser TAPAS €€

9 MAP P114, D1

This little tapas place, not special-looking from outside, is a superior Benimaclet option. It packs out, and no wonder: its *pintxo*-style creations are some of the *barrio's* best, and prices are fair. Food has an ecological focus, and vegetarians are well catered for. Mark your choices on a list, or go to the bar and point. It's best to book. (www.facebook.com/elcarabasser)

Ambra Poble-Bar VALENCIAN €€

10 MAP P114, D1

The front terrace and back garden of this relaxed but professional spot – as much house as restaurant – are great places to absorb Benimaclet life with a drink and some 'Valencian people's cooking'. It has fine rice dishes, plus *coques* (*cocas* in Castilian Spanish;

Las Fallas

The exuberant, anarchic swirl of **Las Fallas de San José** (www.fallas.com) – fireworks, music, festive bonfires and all-night partying – is a must if you're visiting Spain in mid-March. It's one of the country's most notable fiestas.

The *fallas* themselves (*falles* in *valenciano*) are huge sculptural ensembles of wood, papier mâché, polystyrene and other materials built by teams of local artists. Each neighbourhood sponsors its own *falla*, and when the town wakes after the *plantà* (overnight construction of the *fallas*) on 16 March, more than 350 have sprung up. Reaching up to 15m high, with the most expensive costing hundreds of thousands of euros, these grotesque, colourful effigies satirise celebrities, current affairs and local customs. They range from comical to moving and Valencians keenly judge the quality of the individual figures, known as *ninots*, within the ensembles. There are prizes for the best *fallas* in each category, and winning the overall best *falla* prize is a high honour with strenuous competition.

As well as the figures, expect all the trappings of a proper Spanish fiesta. Around-the-clock festivities include brass bands waking the city at 8am, street parties, paella-cooking competitions, parades, open-air concerts, bullfights and fireworks displays. Valencia considers itself the pyrotechnic capital of the world and each day at 2pm from 1 to 19 March, a *mascletà* (over five minutes of deafening thumps and explosions, building to an ear-splitting climax) shakes the window panes of Plaza del Ayuntamiento.

But the major pyrotechnics are yet to come. On the final night, 19 March, all the *fallas* go up in flames – backed by yet more fireworks. So, do all the *ninots* end as charred cinders? All but one: a popular vote spares the most-cherished figure, which gets housed for posterity in the Museo Fallero (p91). It's a good place to get a feel for the *fallas* and the evolution of the festival through the 19th and 20th centuries.

Book accommodation well ahead for Las Fallas. Other towns and villages in the Valencian region also have *fallas* celebrations these days, so it's a great time to be in the area.

Valencia's version of pizza) and *picaetes* (tapas appetisers), several of which make a meal.

Reservations advised for outdoor tables in summer. (www.ambrapoblebar.com)

Que Ganeta Tinc VALENCIAN €€

11 MAP P114, E3

White furniture and big windows give a luminous feel to this amiable restaurant on a bohemian square. It aims more for university staff than students, with beautifully crafted homestyle dishes including salads, desserts, ceviches, fresh fish and steaks. Its well-priced set meals are delicious. (www.queganetatinc.es)

Tanto Monta TAPAS €

12 MAP P114, E3

Legendary, tasty and cheap, this place packs out in the evenings with students, academics and all-comers jostling for a place to enjoy delicious *montaditos* (tapas snacks on bread). Grab a table outside – if you can – and select a mixed plate at the bar. No fighting over who eats what; they're all tops. (www.facebook.com/montaditosvalencia)

Drinking

Deseo 54 LGBTIQ+

13 MAP P114, A1

It's mostly the young and beautiful at this upmarket and famous *discoteca,* which plays pop hits and house to a largely, but not exclusively, LGBTIQ+ crowd. Admission prices vary depending on night and DJ and whether you have a flyer. You can buy tickets online. (www.deseo54.com)

La Salamandra BAR

14 MAP P114, E3

Atmospheric and intimate, this pub is a classic of lively Plaza Xúquer in the university zone. It's a favourite haunt of academics who appreciate a well-poured gin and tonic and music that was recorded years before their students were born, but its terrace is frequented by a younger clientele for evening beers.

Rumbo 144 CLUB

15 MAP P114, F4

Get down with the students on Thursday nights at this uncomplicated university-area nightclub. Chart hits, cheapish drinks, late closing and occasional live acts or DJs make it ever-popular. You'll feel ancient if you're 30. A couple of other nightclubs are opposite. (www.facebook.com/rumbo144vlc)

Entertainment

Valencia Club de Fútbol FOOTBALL

16 MAP P114, D3

The city's principal team, and a major player in Spanish football, with famously demanding fans. A long-planned move to a new ground in the city's northwest won't happen before 2025–26, so for now they're at Mestalla (p115), an atmospheric, steeply tiered ground not far from the city centre. You can buy tickets a few weeks in advance online. (www.valenciacf.com)

La Salà LIVE MUSIC

17 MAP P114, F4

La Salà puts on great live-music nights, with quality performers and a leaning towards world music – cumbia, rocksteady, forró, Balkan, Spanish folk – plus local artists,

Valencian Football

Football is big in Valencia, and going to a game is a great experience. There are two main teams, normally at home on alternate weekends from late August to mid-May. Matches are scheduled any time from Friday night to Monday night, and this is decided a couple of weeks before.

The big brother is Valencia CF, in recent decades one of Spain's more successful teams and winners of numerous Spanish and European trophies. It is one of the world's best supported clubs, with notoriously demanding fans and a strong tradition of developing top players from its own academy.

Levante UD (www.levanteud.com; Estadi Ciutat de València, Calle de San Vicente de Paul 44) has fewer resources, is often beset with financial problems and has recently yo-yoed between the top and second divisions. Nevertheless, though the little sibling, it is the older club, having originated in 1909 in the maritime district of El Cabanyal where it still has strong support.

DJs or cabaret. Music starts around 9.30pm, Thursday or Friday to Sunday. There's space to dance and you can have a cocktail on the terrace. It's Valencia's only live-music venue run by women. (www.lasalavalencia.com)

Matisse Club

LIVE MUSIC

18 MAP P114, F4

This atmospheric and friendly bar and venue has a varied musical program. It has a line-up of talented and inventive musicians, ranging from jazz, soul or funk to flamenco or classical, several nights a week. It's more of a sit-down-and-listen than a get-up-and-dance place. (www.matisseclub.com)

Black Note

LIVE MUSIC

19 MAP P114, D4

One of Valencia's most active live-music venues, reliable Black Note puts on soul, jazz, pop-rock, blues or R&B every Wednesday to Saturday night, from around 11pm. Admission prices vary, depending who's grooving. Wednesday- and Thursday-night jam sessions are fun. (www.blacknoteclub.com)

16 Toneladas

LIVE MUSIC

20 MAP P114, A1

This spacious venue down the side of the bus station has regular live acts – rock, soul, new wave and more, with many international visitors – and also functions as a nightclub. (www.16toneladas.com)

Explore

Valencia's Seaside

Valencia's city beach is 4km from the centre. A very broad strip of sand nearly 4km long, it's bordered by the Paseo Marítimo promenade and strings of restaurants and cafes. The refurbished port and marina area, a stop for cruise ships, is south of here and backed by the intriguing old fishers' district of El Cabanyal, which makes for excellent exploration and has some great eating options.

The Short List

- ***Playa de la Patacona (p125)*** *Relaxing at the beach, gazing over the Mediterranean towards the Balearic Islands.*
- ***Cabanyal eating (p123)*** *Sampling fresh local seafood in traditional taverns like Casa Montaña.*
- ***La Fábrica de Hielo (p128)*** *Dancing the afternoon away at this artsy-bohemian beachside music spot.*
- ***Mercat Municipal del Cabanyal (p123)*** *Appraising the produce on offer before taking a stroll around the barrio.*

Getting There & Around

Lines 4 and 6 head out to the beaches and El Cabanyal.

M Take line 5 or 7 to Marítim station then change to tram line 8 to Neptú for the marina area and southern Cabanyal.

From the Ciutat Vella bus 31 is good for the northern half of the beach strip, and 32 for Cabanyal and the southern half.

Valencia Cabanyal station is 15 minutes from the Estación del Norte on *cercanías* trains.

Neighbourhood Map on p124

Playa de la Malvarrosa (p125)

Walking Tour

Strolling Through El Cabanyal

El Cabanyal, traditionally a fishers' quarter, is full of working-class maritime character with its narrow, straight streets dotted with quirky tiled facades. In the 2000s Cabanyal fought off a city-hall plan to drive a major road through its heart to the beach. Since then, community-driven cultural initiatives and an ever-improving bar and restaurant scene are helping revive the barrio.

Start Mercado Municipal del Cabanyal

Finish Bodega La Peseta

Length 1.5km; one hour

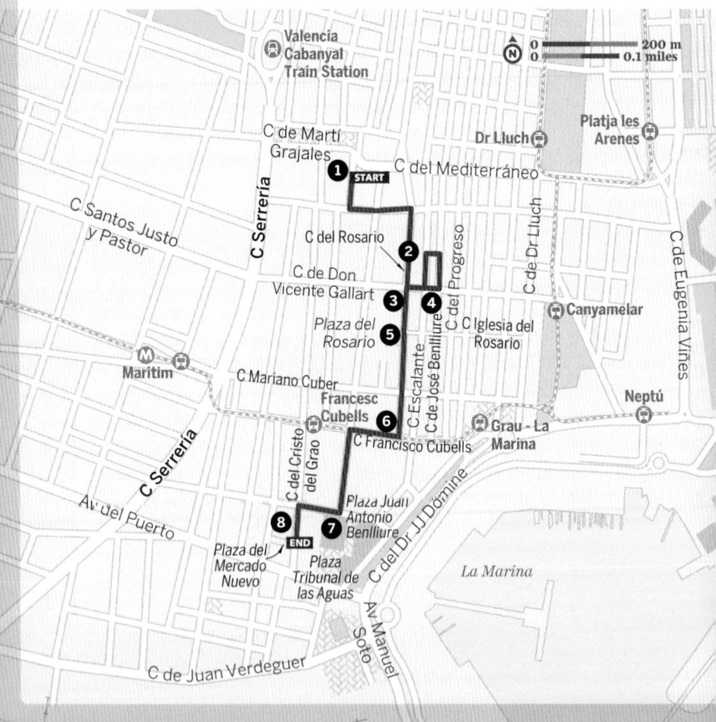

❶ Local Market

Start at the **Mercat Municipal del Cabanyal** (www.mercadocabanyal.es). Sturdy old ladies jostle each other and suspiciously prod the vegetables in this vibrant, well-stocked, local food market.

❷ Narrow Streets

Wander southeast into the core of the district. The narrow streets are flanked by some of Cabanyal's pretty centenarian houses, decorated with colourful tiling and fancy mouldings – vernacular versions of the grand Modernista mansions in richer parts of town.

❸ Street Art

At the corner of Calles Rosario and Gaillart you can't miss a particularly fine piece of Valencian street art – a multi-painter tribute to artist José Segrelles (1885–1969).

❹ Historic Tavern

With venerable barrels and the atmosphere of another era, **Bodega Casa Montaña** (www.emilianobodega.com) has been around since 1836. It has a superb, changing selection of wines and exquisite tapas (bookings advised).

❺ Plaza del Rosario

This palm-shaded square is a nice place to sit and watch *barrio* life pass by. It's dominated by the local church's facade, with the community theatre next door. Just down the street, stop for a drink at inviting little **Bar Lapaca** (p127).

❻ Rice Museum

Restored rice mill **Museo del Arroz** (www.museodelarrozdevalencia.com) has three levels of complex belts, pulleys and machinery to enthrall those of an engineering bent.

❼ Gothic Shipyards

Built in the 14th century, the Gothic-style **Atarazanas** (www.valencia.es/cas/la-ciudad/museos) are shipbuilding warehouses that have been altered over the years. The beautifully restored interior, with five parallel naves and arches like a whale's ribs, holds temporary exhibitions.

❽ Tapas Time

Next to the **Mercado Municipal del Grao** (Plaza del Mercado Nuevo), **Bodega La Peseta** (www.facebook.com/bodegalapeseta.elgraovalencia;) is a Cabanyal '70s-retro-style alternative icon. It has tasty tapas (tortillas are its speciality) and decent wines and vermouth.

A B C D
1 2 3 4 5 6

0 500 m
0 0.25 miles

For reviews see

Sights	p125
Eating	p125
Drinking	p128
Entertainment	p129

19
Av Mare Mostrum
Av Mare Nostrum
Paseo Marítimo de la Patacona
1 *Playa de la Patacona*
7
C Gran Canaria
Av Malvarrosa
13
C de José Ballester Gozalvo
C de Isabel de Villena
C San Rafael
Playa de la Malvarrosa
3
Beteró
Av Naranjos
C Rio Tajo
Platja Malvarrosa
Golfo de Valencia
La Cadena
C Remonta
16
10
C de Eugenia Viñes
21
C Luis Peixo
Cabanyal
C Pintor Ferrandis
C Reina
20
17
Valencia Cabanyal Train Station
6 *Bodega J Flor*
C Escalante
C Pescadores
C de Martí Grajales
Dr Lluch
Platja les Arenes
C del Mediterráneo
C de José Benlliure
12
C del Rosario
C de Don Vicente Gallart
9
C del Progreso
C de Barraca
C de Dr Lluch
2 *Playa de las Arenas*
C de Eugenia Viñes
Paseo de Neptuno
Canyamelar
C Serrería
Plaza del Rosario 22
15
14
11
8
AC Park
C Iglesia del Rosario
Marítim
C Mariano Cuber
Grau - La Marina
Neptú
18
C Francisco Cubells
Francesc Cubells
C del Dr JJ Dòmine
Plaza Juan Antonio Benlliure
4 Mundomarino
Marina Real Juan Carlos I
5 Rent Yacht World
Av del Puerto
Plaza Tribunal de las Aguas
La Marina
C de Juan Verdeguer
Av Manuel Soto

Sights

Playa de la Patacona BEACH

1 MAP P124, C1

The northern stretch of Valencia's city beach has a quiet, local scene than stretches further south. It's backed by lovely traditional houses – some have been converted into eateries. Several appealing *chiringuito* (beach-bar) options are on the sand. Patacona gets busy in summer, but like the rest of the strip, it's a wide, flat beach with plenty of room to move even in high season.

Playa de las Arenas BEACH

2 MAP P124, C5

Stretching north from the marina, this is the closest part of Valencia's city beach to the centre, and the focal point of seaside life. Backed by hotels and rice restaurants, it's a lively, busy strip with a lot of summer nightlife nearby. The beach is over 100m deep, so there's room to move even in high summer.

Playa de la Malvarrosa BEACH

3 MAP P124, C3

The middle section of the main beach is popular with joggers and cyclists for its promenade. It's a halfway house between busier Las Arenas beach to its south and quieter Patacona to the north. There's plenty of space on the wide stretch of sand, but eating and drinking choices are less abundant.

Mundomarino BOATING

4 MAP P124, C6

Offers a variety of catamaran excursions, from sailing (one/three hours€15/42) to sunset cruises (€22) and swimming trips (€20). (www.mundomarino.es)

Rent Yacht World BOATING

5 MAP P124, D6

With a skipper who is serious about both safety and fun, this is a great option for a few people to get out on a yacht. You can book private trips for two to 11 people, including fuel and a drink, from one hour to a whole day. It also rents out self-drive motorboats, and speedboats for those with a licence. Other options might see you take to the Med for a week or more, cruising over to the Balearic Islands. (www.rentyachtworld.es)

Eating

Bar Cabanyal SEAFOOD €€

6 MAP P124, A4

Opposite the market in the traditional fishing district, you'd expect a marine flavour, and indeed the young and enthusiastic team does an excellent line in quality seafood at reasonable prices. Everything is delicious at this upbeat, optimistic spot. Try *esgarraet*, a Valencian salad of red peppers and salt cod, followed by squid or octopus, then cake. (www.facebook.com/bar cabanyal)

Almuerzo – A Valencian Rite

In much of the Spanish-speaking world, *almuerzo* is a word for lunch. But for Valencians, it's a midmorning bite – called *esmorzaret* in *valenciano* – and often a substantial one. Head to traditional bars to experience it – **Bodega J Flor** (www.restaurantebodegaflor.es), Casa Guillermo and La Pascuala in Cabanyal are typical – and see people downing *bocadillos* (filled rolls) as long as your forearm, or maybe a plate of calamari, accompanied by peanuts, lupin beans and a beer or two. Then a coffee and it's back to work. So it's a kind of brunch? No, because they'll have lunch afterwards too!

La Más Bonita

CAFE **€€**

7 MAP P124, B2

Pretty in turquoise and white and perfectly situated on the Patacona beachfront, La Más Bonita has comfy seating out front, a contemporary vibe, a big interior and a long, cool garden-patio. Ideal for breakfast or brunch, its long menu includes pancakes, egg dishes, granola, fruit and hard-to-resist homemade cake. Also good for light meals or drinks. Book in summer, even for breakfast. There's also a *chiringuito* (beach bar) on the sand. (www.lamasbonita.es)

La Llimera

TAPAS **€€**

8 MAP P124, B5

La Llimera has an eclectic range of well-prepared plates (two or three make a meal), and three appealing spaces to enjoy them: a whitewashed brick interior (can be noisy), a shaded garden patio and a terrace on the quiet plaza behind. Food runs from hummus and baked aubergines to inventive salads (one with quinoa), tasty homemade meatballs and duck *à l'orange* cannelloni.

Save room for Atrevido dessert – chocolate truffles with a flask of peppery homemade limoncello. Service by the young, multinational team is rapid and there's a great selection of well-priced wines. Reservations advised. (www.facebook.com/llimeracabanyal)

Bodega Anyora

TAPAS **€€**

9 MAP P124, A5

Old Valencia through a modern design eye, rehabilitated Anyora is a charming tavern, with gleaming handmade tiles, hanging herbs and fresco vegetables on the walls. It does snacks to accompany a vermouth as well as quality plates, rooted in local produce and tradition with modern twists. Food fanatics could try cockscombs, pig's ear or snout.

It has plenty of good wines by the bottle or glass, mostly natural or organic. Try the weekday lunchtime set menus. Reservations advised. (www.anyora.es)

La Pascuala

SANDWICHES €

10 MAP P124, B4

Large and legendary La Pascuala is famed for huge *bocadillos* that come stuffed with fillings. Half of Valencia seems to be here at 11am for a midmorning bite. There's a huge selection; the Merche (omelette, pork and goat's cheese) is fairly typical size-wise. A *medio* (half) is enough for most non-Valencians. (www.facebook.com/bodegalapascuala)

Casa Guillermo

TAPAS €€

11 MAP P124, B5

This Cabanyal tapas spot is renowned for tasty but rather pricey anchovies – have them as a shared starter. Other dishes, such as croquettes, mini-burgers or mussels, are also delicious and more compassionately priced. It's small, so lunch or dinner reservations are essential.

You can also have anchovies as the filling for a midmorning *bocadillo*. (www.casaguillermo1957.com)

Ca la Mar

TAPAS €

12 MAP P124, B5

Informal and down to earth, this neighbourhood gem is typical of the Cabanyal district. There's a cheerful scene at the outdoor tables, with tasty seafood and other tapas at knockdown prices. (www.facebook.com/calamarcabanyal)

Casa Carmela

VALENCIAN €€

13 MAP P124, B2

Family-favourite Casa Carmela's paellas are among Valencia's best. The expansive restaurant has served rice since 1922. Huge paellas are cooked over an orange-wood fire and eaten with spoons. It's open lunchtime only, Tuesday to Saturday; reservations are a good idea. Order ahead for traditional *paella valenciana* (with chicken and/or rabbit, snails and green beans). There's a minimum table spend of €40 per person. (www.casa-carmela.com)

Bar Lapaca

TAPAS €

14 MAP P124, B5

Cosy and buzzing Lapaca has a varied crowd and uplifting atmosphere. Visually striking with chessboard tiles and deep reds, it does simple, tasty tapas (including some vegetarian options) and craft beers at fair prices. (www.instagram.com/barlapaca)

Ca la Mar

PENNY KIDD/LONELY PLANET

La Sastrería VALENCIAN €€€

15 MAP P124, B5

In a former Cabanyal tailor's shop cleverly done up in check tiles, ceramics and maritime blue, La Sastrería provides contemporary preparations of maritime local produce. You will eat well, and service is attentive, though prices seem a little elevated. It's popular: booking is near-essential. In the restaurant you can observe the chefs hard at work in the open kitchen. (www.lasastreriavalencia.com)

La Lonja del Pescado SEAFOOD €€

16 MAP P124, B4

One block back from the Malvarrosa beach, this busy, informal place has plenty of atmosphere. It specialises in traditional fried seafood and fish at decent value. Take an order form as you enter and fill it in at your table. Platja Malva-rosa tram stop is right outside. (www.facebook.com/lalonja.delpescado)

Marina Beach Club.

Drinking

La Fábrica de Hielo CAFE, BAR

17 MAP P124, B4

A former ice factory, converted with charm into a sizeable multipurpose space with music, drinks, tapas and other cultural goings-on (dance, film, theatre, circus...) just back from the beach. It has an artsy-bohemian vibe and there's usually live music (jazz to hip-hop, flamenco to blues) Wednesday, Saturday and Sunday nights and Sunday lunchtime. Guest DJs Friday nights. (www.lafabricadehielo.net)

Marina Beach Club BAR

18 MAP P124, C5

A super-popular beach club with two restaurants, a pool, bar and nightclub, in an enviable spot between Valencia's marina and Playa de las Arenas. The open-air space has palm trees and great beach views. A hit with locals and visitors, it gets crowded in the height of summer, so book ahead (different sections require separate bookings). (www.marinabeachclub.com)

La Casa de la Mar BAR

19 MAP P124, B1

This cavernous warehouse a block from Patacona beach is a great music venue, with live acts just about every evening and some weekend afternoons. There's a well-stocked drinks bar, a gourmet burger bar and a party atmosphere. Also here are the changing rooms, showers and lockers of Mediterranean Surf (p29). (www.lacasadelamar.com)

La Batisfera

BAR

20 MAP P124, B4

This family-friendly space combines an upbeat bar-cafe, which often has live music and other events, with a bookshop possessing a great new-and-used novels selection (in English). (www.facebook.com/labatisfera.cafeterialibreria)

Akuarela Playa

CLUB

21 MAP P124, B4

A huge space in a historic villa complex, this typical summer nightclub has a large outdoor terrace. Just across the street from Malvarrosa beach, it's a classic of the Valencian hot season. The music is commercial – mainly Spanish and Latin pop. You can buy tickets (€20 including a drink) online. (www.akuarelaplaya.es)

Entertainment

Teatre El Musical

THEATRE

22 MAP P124, A5

With an outrageously tall door and modern interior, this theatre in the heart of the Cabanyal *barrio* has a busy community-involved program of theatre, dance, music, poetry and comedy, with some events OK for young children. (www.teatreelmusical.es)

Top Spots for Valencian Almuerzo

Alenar Bodega Mediterránea In this city-centre bar everything revolves around good produce and Mediterranean wines and plates with an eye to the Marina Alta district: gastronomy with roots.

Bodega J Flor If you love authentic locales with tradition, don't miss the *bocadillo* filled with oyster mushrooms, sausage, fried egg and fried potatoes in this Cabanyal bar.

Bar Mercado de Ruzafa Valencian *almuerzo* is essence and tradition. There's nowhere better to live the experience than a bar with market ambience in the city's most modern neighbourhood.

Bar Nuevo Oslo Almuerzo is all about gastronomic hedonism and this bar near Àngel Guimerà metro has the most spectacular counter display in the city.

By Joan Ruiz, *bar hunter and food lover @esmorzaret*

Explore

Western Valencia

There are several good reasons to head into the broad swath of suburbs that spreads west of the old town. At the western end of the Turia riverbed, the Bioparc zoo presents African animals in innovative ways, while the city history museum gives a good overview of Valencia's past. A few of the city's most enjoyable restaurants are here, and a number of green spaces give a pleasant change of pace from inner-city life.

The Short List

- ***Bioparc (p133)*** *Getting up close and personal with the lemurs at this unusual zoo devoted to African animals.*
- ***Jardín Botánico (p133)*** *Strolling peacefully around this fairly central green space run by the University of Valencia.*
- ***Rausell (p133)*** *Savouring a bar or restaurant meal at one of Valencia's most beloved locales.*

Getting There & Around

The area is served by many buses, including the 95, which runs along the north side of the Turia riverbed to the bridge near the Bioparc, then along the south side heading back east.

M The closest stop to the Bioparc and history museum is Nou d'Octubre.

The bike lanes of the Turia riverbed get you close to many points of interest.

Neighbourhood Map on p132

Jardín Botánico (p133) JOAN_BAUTISTA/SHUTTERSTOCK©

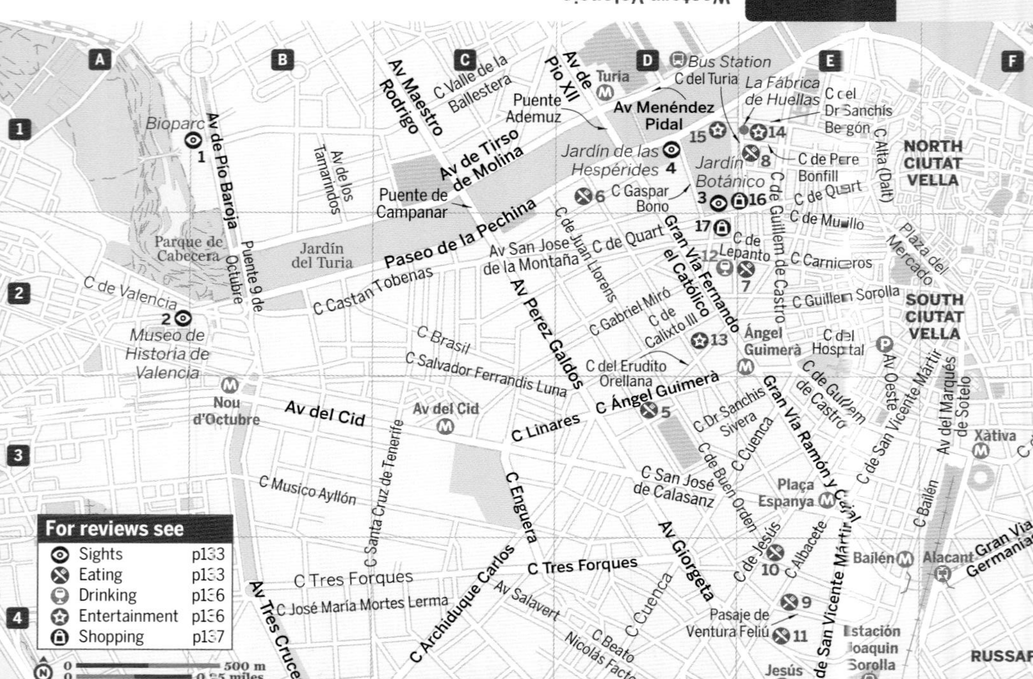
For reviews see
Sights p133
Eating p133
Drinking p136
Entertainment p136
Shopping p137
0 500 m
0 0.25 miles
NORTH CIUTAT VELLA
SOUTH CIUTAT VELLA
RUSSAFA
Bus Station
C del Turia
La Fábrica de Huellas
Av Menéndez Pidal
Turia
Av de Pío XII
Puente Ademuz
Av de Tirso de Molina
Puente de Campanar
Av Maestro Rodrigo
C Valle de la Ballestera
Av de los Tamarindos
Jardín del Turia
Paseo de la Pechina
Puente 9 de Octubre
Av de Pío Baroja
Bioparc
Parque de Cabecera
C de Valencia
Museo de Historia de Valencia
Nou d'Octubre
Av del Cid
C Castan Tobenas
Av San Jose de la Montaña
C de Juan Llorens
C de Quart
C Gaspar Bono
Jardín de las Hespérides
Jardín Botánico
C de Pere Bonfill
C de Quart
C Alta (Dalt)
C del Dr Sanchis Bergón
C de Guillem de Castro
C de Murillo
C Carniceros
C Guillem Sorolla
C de Lepanto
Plaza del Mercado
Gran Vía Fernando el Católico
C Gabriel Miró
C de Calixto III
C del Erudito Orellana
C Ángel Guimerà
Ángel Guimerà
C del Hospital
Av Oeste
C de Guillem de Castro
Gran Vía Ramón y Cajal
Av Perez Galdos
C Brasil
C Salvador Ferrandis Luna
C Linares
Av del Cid
C Dr Sanchis Sivera
C Cuenca
C de Buen Orden
C San José de Calasanz
Plaça Espanya
C de Jesús
C Albacete
C de San Vicente Mártir
Av del Marqués de Sotelo
Xàtiva
C de Colón
C Bailén
Bailén
Alacant
Gran Vía Germanias
Av Giorgeta
Pasaje de Ventura Feliu
Estación Joaquín Sorolla
Jesús
C Cuenca
C Beato Nicolás Factor
C Enguera
C Tres Forques
C Archiduque Carlos
Av Salavert
C Santa Cruz de Tenerife
C Musico Ayllón
C Tres Forques
C José María Mortes Lerma
Av Tres Cruces

Sights

Bioparc

ZOO

1 MAP P132, B1

This zoo devoted to African animals has an educational and conservationist remit, with over 100 endangered species, and an unusual approach. Though, as always, confinement of creatures like gorillas in limited spaces raises mixed feelings, the innovative landscaping is certainly thrilling. The absence of obvious fences makes it seem that animals roam free as you wander from savannah to equatorial landscapes. Aardvarks, leopards and hippos draw crowds, but most magical is Madagascar, where large-eyed lemurs gambol around your feet among waterfalls and grass. (www.bioparcvalencia.es)

Museo de Historia de Valencia

MUSEUM

2 MAP P132, A2

The Valencia History Museum, set in an atmospheric, crypt-like, 19th-century water deposit, is well-presented and plots more than 2000 years of Valencia's history in interesting but not excessive detail. Each period is illustrated with a display case, making the visit a little like window shopping. Posted information is in Spanish and *valenciano*, but some of the displays have touchscreens which activate short films in a choice of languages, illustrating the life of the period in question. (http://mhv.valencia.es)

Jardín Botánico

GARDENS

3 MAP P132, D1

Established in 1802, this walled garden run by the University of Valencia was Spain's first botanic garden. With mature trees and plants, an extensive cactus garden and a wary colony of feral cats (which we're asked not to feed or touch), it's a shady, tranquil place to relax. Check the website for evening jazz concerts. (www.jardibotanic.org)

Jardín de las Hespérides

GARDENS

4 MAP P132, D1

The small modern garden abutting the botanical garden could not be more distinct in style. Shorter on green space, it has the formality of a classic French garden with cypress trees, low banks of herbs and staggered terraces where tangy citrus trees flourish. (www.jardins.valencia.es)

Eating

Rausell

VALENCIAN **€€**

5 MAP P132, D3

With three-quarters of a century and three generations of one family behind it, Rausell is loved by locals for its fabulous tapas and meals – harbour-fresh seafood, succulent cuts of meat, perfect rice dishes. Sit at the bar or bar tables, or in the dining room.

It's open nearly all day Wednesday to Saturday (9am to 5pm Sunday), so good for breakfast or early lunch. Service is top-notch, both friendly and attentive. There's a super-popular takeaway section adjoining the restaurant if you fancy a freshly spit-roasted chicken, a kilo or two of paella or many other options. (www.rausell.es)

Bar Ricardo

TAPAS €€

6 MAP P132, D1

Ice-cold beer and a fabulous array of tapas and other dishes characterise this gloriously traditional place, with its old-style mezzanine, pleasant terrace and top-notch service. Snails, quality seafood, some of Valencia's best *patatas bravas* (fried potatoes in spicy sauce) and other delights await. The kitchen is open all day, so it's a good spot for eating outside normal Spanish hours. (www.barricardo.es)

Pelegrí

SPANISH €€

7 MAP P132, E2

A little off the centre's tourist beat, this refined spot makes a fine lunch or dinner venue. The parents-and-daughter team offer four set menus and a short à la carte menu that are brilliant value for food that's beautifully conceived and presented without losing the comfort factor. Interesting wines round out the meal. (www.restaurantepelegrivalencia.com)

La Greta

TAPAS €

8 MAP P132, E1

In an eye-catching and original environment – all quirky retro design – La Greta has a pleasing menu of tapas and plates designed to share, with lots of vegetarian choice and bits of Lebanese and Indian influence. Portions are generous and service welcoming.

El Pederniz

SPANISH €€

9 MAP P132, E4

A warm welcome and lots of enthusiasm give a great first impression at this comfortably decorated restaurant that makes a pleasant surprise in a nondescript area. Delicious seafood and game dishes make for an excellent experience. It's worth seeking out even if you're not heading to or from the nearby Joaquín Sorolla train station. (www.facebook.com/restauranteelpederniz)

Pastelería Dulce de Leche

CAFE €

10 MAP P132, E4

Always busy, this patisserie-cafe does a splendid range of delicious cakes, tarts and other baked goods; it's pretty tough to choose. There are also decent savoury options including pasta. Order at the counter, then take your number to a table. (www.pasteleriadulcedeleche.com)

Mercado San Vicente

MARKET €€

11 MAP P132, E4

This has been under construction for a few years, but will hopefully be open by the time you get there. It's a new gastro-market designed along the lines of Madrid's famous Mercado San Miguel. Stalls in the former printing factory near Joaquín Sorolla train station will sell quality produce and provide tapas.

Valencia: A Brief History of the City

Pensioned-off Roman legionaries founded 'Valentia' on the banks of the Río Turia in 138 BCE. The city was destroyed by Pompey in 75 BCE during the Sertorian War, a Roman civil war fought on the Iberian Peninsula, but began to revive about 50 years later.

The Moors made 'Balansiya' an agricultural and industrial centre, establishing ceramics, paper, silk and leather industries and extending irrigation canals into the fertile hinterland. Muslim rule was briefly interrupted in 1094 CE by the triumphant rampage of legendary Castilian knight El Cid. The Christian forces of Jaime I, King of Aragón, took the city in 1238 after a siege. Tens of thousands of Muslims were displaced. Jaime made the Valencia region a kingdom with its own laws, the *fueros*.

Valencia's golden age was the 15th and early 16th centuries, when it became a major Mediterranean trading centre and the biggest city on the Iberian Peninsula. Commerce brought wealth and magnificent buildings. However, the expulsion of the Jews, then the *moriscos* (converted Muslims), from Spain left it bereft of important sectors of society. Meanwhile, New World discoveries led to a Spanish pivot towards the Atlantic, beginning Sevilla's pre-eminence as a trading city and hastening Valencia's decline. Economic hardship led to the Germanías revolt (1519–22) of the guilds and peasants against the Church and aristocracy. Lean centuries ensued, finally relieved in the 19th century by industrialisation and the development of a lucrative citrus trade to northern Europe. The *fueros* were abolished in 1707 as Madrid tightened control over Spanish regions.

Loyalist Valencia was the capital of republican Spain for nearly a year (1936–37) during the Spanish Civil War, after the government abandoned Madrid. In the war's traumatic final days, the city surrendered and a period of harsh repression and poverty ensued, not helped by severe floods in 1949 and 1957 that led to the Río Turia being diverted away from the city centre. An economic upturn in the 1960s, based on industry, tourism and services, brought many immigrants from other parts of Spain and apartment-block suburbs sprang up to house them.

The return to democracy in 1975 brought regional semi-autonomy and a huge injection of confidence to Valencia. Though the city went bankrupt in the global financial crisis, a casualty of corruption and overborrowing, things are on the up, the city is more multicultural than ever, and the vibrancy of daily life here is always remarkable.

Drinking

Pub Bubu

GAY

12 MAP P132, D2

Haven't shaved since the holiday started? Not a problem at all here at this notably friendly bear den. The inclusive atmosphere makes anybody feel at home. There's usually a guest DJ on Friday nights. (www.facebook.com/pubbubu)

Entertainment

Loco Club

LIVE MUSIC

13 MAP P132, D2

Popular, long-established Loco puts on a continuous stream of Spanish and international bands and solo acts, usually between Thursday and Sunday. Rock and related genres are the main staples but you'll also get some soul, country and indie performers. (www.lococlub.es)

Café del Duende

LIVE PERFORMANCE

14 MAP P132, E1

Intimate Café del Duende stages decent-quality, reasonably authentic flamenco performances four nights a week. It's quite small and doesn't take reservations, so it's worth queueing before the show starts to avoid disappointment. Shows last about an hour. (www.cafedelduende.com)

Cake display, Pastelería Dulce de Leche (p134)

Coffee in a Cat Colony

Missing a feline companion from back home? Or you just like cats? **La Fábrica de Huellas** (www.lafabricadehuellas.com; Calle del Turia 60) is for you. At this cafe, part of the animal-therapy-focused Fundación Acavall, you can enjoy an organic coffee, infusion, smoothie or snack in the 'Casa de los Gatos', an impeccably clean, well-appointed room housing a dozen or two cats available for adoption. Reservations are advised for these very popular afternoon (and weekend morning) sessions. The front section of the cafe, meanwhile, is a dog-friendly space where your canine can accompany you as you eat, drink and chat. Sensibly, the cats and dogs are kept well apart!

Teatro la Estrella — PUPPET THEATRE

15 MAP P132, D1

This puppet theatre puts on weekend shows aimed at families. It's an enchanting spot, and you can see some of the puppets displayed beforehand. Many of the shows are based on well-known fairy tales. Some are more suited to non-Spanish-speaking kids than others, so it's best to ask first. It runs another theatre in the Cabanyal district near the beach. (Sala Petxina; www.teatrolaestrella.com)

Shopping

Vinyl Eye — CLOTHING

16 MAP P132, E1

This cool shop has a range of prints with original designs inspired by music, cinema, cycling and more, including many by noted Valencia street artists like Disneylexya and David Limón. Different edgy artists exhibit here. Get T-shirts, tote bags and sweatshirts printed in five minutes with any motifs you like or from your own photos. You can order online too. (www.vinyl-eye.com)

Botànic — TEA, COFFEE

17 MAP P132, D2

A neat little shop opposite the Jardín Botánico entrance, specialising in single-origin tea and coffee from around the world. It has over 100 kinds of tea – black, green, red, white, aromatic, flavoured, relaxing, even blue – ranged in tins on the shop shelves, and freshly roasted 100% Arabica coffee from about 10 countries, which they can grind according to your needs. Also has assorted pots, tins, percolators, grinders and a few jams and chutneys. (www.botaniccafete.com)

Walking Tour

The Turia Riverbed

Congratulate the citizen campaigners who, when the Río Turia was diverted after a devastating 1957 flood, fought to make the riverbed into a park instead of a motorway. The glorious park is busy any time of day with strollers, cyclists, joggers, dog-walkers, playgrounders and romancers. It's a great snapshot of everyday Valencian life and a relief from concrete, stone and traffic; it's worth walking its full 9km length.

Start Ciudad de las Artes y las Ciencias

Finish Parque de Cabecera

Length 9km; two to 2½ hours

Bus 35 takes you to the park's southern end from the Estación del Norte.

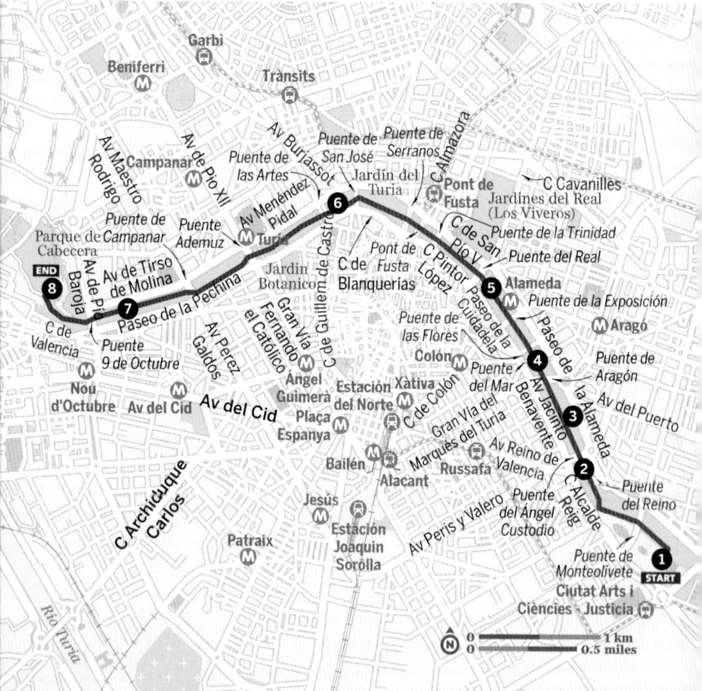

❶ Getting Active

Start your walk at the magnificent **Ciudad de las Artes y las Ciencias** (p86). But will it be a walk? There's also cycle hire or a continuous running track with built-in gradients and distance markers. Regularly spaced public exercise machines are another way to work off the tapas.

❷ Gulliver

While the whole of the Turia could be considered Valencia's playground, there's nothing to compare with the giant **Gulliver**, which begs to be clambered over. This giant recumbent man has ropes to climb, slides and more. It's a lovely scene for young kids, with an adjacent skate park to keep the older ones happy.

❸ Musical Landmark

City landmark, **Palau de la Música** (www.palauvalencia.com), perched over the dry riverbed, is an attractive concert hall hosting mainly classical concerts. That long glass tube looks good but can get pretty hot on a summer's day.

❹ Beautiful Bridges

One of the most attractive of the Turia's old bridges, the elegant Renaissance span of the **Puente del Mar** was commissioned in 1591; pride of place goes to images of the Virgin Mary and St Pascual Baylón. Shortly beyond, the **Puente de las Flores** is decorated with 27,000 flowerpots.

❺ Greenery

The stretch between the **Puente de la Exposición** and the **Puente de la Trinidad**, passing under the Puente del Real, is green and shady, with mature trees from oranges and palms to poplars and jacarandas. You can almost imagine you're in the countryside!

❻ The Oval Ball

While soccer grabs the headlines, rugby also has a devoted following here. The ground with the finest setting is here in the riverbed.

❼ Watercourses

Water lore is a major part of Valencian culture, and the eight *acequias* (irrigation canals) diverting water from the Río Turia to keep the market gardens watered are legendary. At former weir **Azud de Rovella** you can see where the last of them, the Acequia de Rovella, was diverted into a channel on concrete legs.

❽ City Parkland

At the end of Turia park, landscaped **Parque de Cabecera** has a grassy mound to climb for views, plus paths along a stream connecting two lakes. Take a jaunt in a swan-shaped pedalo and listen for animal sounds from the adjacent **Bioparc** (p133).

Worth a Trip
Wander the Waters of La Albufera

Synonymous with rice, agriculture and the goodness of Valencian soil, the Albufera lagoon and surrounding flatlands sit just south of Valencia city. Long used for rice cultivation, the easily accessed area is the spiritual home of paella and similar dishes. It has important dune and wetland ecosystems and its rural ambience, sea beaches, birdwatching and ricey restaurants make it a great escape.

El Saler

Low-key El Saler village, between Valencia and the Albufera lake, is less than 1km from the seemingly endless Playa del Saler. The beach has a welcome natural feel, backed by a strip of dunes and woodlands, the Devesa de l'Albufera, with several themed walking trails. The village has a line of restaurants and more are near the beach. **Visit Albufera** (www.visitalbufera.com; Avenida Pinares 6, El Saler) runs boat trips to the lake and hires bicycles.

Mirador El Pujol

This **viewpoint** (CV500, Km 9.5) on the main Albufera lake specially comes into its own at sunset, when it's gloriously romantic, with herons slowly flapping against the reddening sky. The Gola del Pujol channel flows out of the lake towards the sea here. You can take lagoon boat trips, including at sunset.

Birdwatching

Birdwatching is good across the area. Around 90 bird species regularly nest here and more than 250 others halt here on their migrations. The **Centro de Interpretación Racó de l'Olla** (www.parquesnaturales.gva.es; Carretera El Palmar, Km 0), just after the turnoff to El Palmar from the CV500, has some information on species, an observation tower and a path to a bird-watching hide.

El Palmar

The most emblematic of the Albufera settlements, this farming village prides itself as being the birthplace of the Valencian rice dish, and these days every second building seems to be a restaurant serving it: it's easy to end up with a bellyful. Boat excursions leaving from here typically last 45 minutes.

★ Top Tips

- Rice is a lunch dish, so time your visit around it. Start your day at the beach, then a rice lunch, trail walk in the Devesa de l'Albufera, evening birdwatching and a sunset boat trip.

Take a Break

There are many rice restaurants, especially in El Palmar. **Arrocería Maribel** (www.arroceriamaribel.com; Calle de Francisco Monleón 5, El Palmar) has paellas and other rice dishes, plus Valencian favourites and vegan options. Reservations advised. Order rice dishes in advance.

★ Getting There

Bus 24 (hourly) and 25 (half-hourly) from Valencia's Plaza Porta de la Mar run to El Saler and Mirador del Pujol. The 24 continues to El Palmar.

A cycle lane from Valencia to El Saler and the flat Albufera terrain make cycling a top option.

Worth a Trip

Take in the Views from Sagunto's Hilltop Castle

Sagunto, 25km north of Valencia, offers spectacular panoramas over orange groves to the coast and the Balearic Islands from its castle, whose long stone walls girdle twin hilltops. A new visitor centre, opened here in 2022, is a big help in understanding the castle's history and the fairly ruinous layout within its walls. With a few pleasant spots to take lunch in the town below the castle, Sagunto makes a good day trip from Valencia.

www.sagunto turismo.com

A Long History

The castle's history began with a thriving Iberian community called (infelicitously, with hindsight) Arse. In 219 BCE Hannibal destroyed it, sparking the Second Punic War. Rome won, named the town Saguntum and rebuilt it. It was the Moors who gave the castle its current form; it was later embellished by the Christians and fought over in the Peninsular War.

The Western Hilltop

The path up from the visitor centre leads into the middle of the castle. Turn right for the western hilltop, which was the site of the original Iberian town. What's here today is mostly later fortifications from the 18th and 19th centuries.

Carved Stones

Between the two hilltops, the Anticuario Epigráfico is a collection of engraved stones found on the site. There are Latin funerary and honorary inscriptions and a few in Hebrew from the medieval era. There's interesting information on Roman customs, but it's not in English.

The Eastern Hilltop

The Roman town and the Moorish citadel were here. In the Plaza de Armas, the heart of the medieval Christian castle, the ruins of the Roman forum have been laid bare. Disappointingly, the columned building beside it only dates from the 20th century. The impressive Almenara gate leads into the area called Plaza de Almenara, which was the Moorish citadel.

Restored Theatre

Below the castle, you can visit the Roman theatre. An overzealous restoration has resulted in an enormous new stage and backdrop, and plastic seating, which are great for staging performances, but short on historical atmosphere.

★ Top Tips

- Pick up a map-leaflet in the visitor centre so you can understand what's what as you explore the castle.

Take a Break

There are no food or refreshments at the castle but there's a bunch of restaurants on the road winding up to the castle from the town centre. **La Taverna de la Serp**, just below the Roman theatre, is good for tapas. Or reserve a tasting menu of creative Mediterranean fare at Michelin-starred **Arrels**.

★ Getting There

Cercanías trains from Valencia's Estación del Norte run at least hourly to Sagunto (one-way €3.70, 30 to 40 minutes). From Sagunto station it's a 1.2km walk to the castle entrance.

Access to the castle is difficult because of a residents' zone, so be prepared to walk up.

Worth a Trip

Uncover Layers of History at Xàtiva

The long, narrow castle stretched along a ridge above Xàtiva, 60km south of Valencia, has a lot of history and offers inspiring views. Though it has been much modified over the years, the layers of history here are evident, and the precinct has an appealingly Mediterranean feel, with sunbaked stone, olives and pine trees on the rocky hill. The ticket office hands out a useful map-leaflet.

www.xativaturismo.com

Castillo Mayor

Ahead of you as you enter the castle, the Castillo Mayor stretches away and upwards along the hilltop. It was first fortified by the Romans, who connected it to the older Castillo Menor (to your left) with walls. If you think it's big today, imagine what it must have looked like 300 years ago at full size. Sadly, it was badly damaged by an earthquake in 1748.

Sala de los Borjas

In the same building as the Talaia del Castell restaurant, two rooms hold an interesting exhibition on the famous Borja (Borgia) dynasty (particularly the popes), who hailed originally from Xàtiva.

Prison

The lockup where Jaume, Count of Urgell, died is one of the castle's most evocative spaces, a vaulted dungeon with no natural light and clearly little hope of escape. The count was only one of a long line of nobles who found themselves detained here during some turbulent centuries in Aragonese dynastic politics.

Torre de la Fe

Literally the high point of the castle, the Tower of Faith offers stunning vistas on both sides and was the heart of the upper castle. From here, the ridge continues to a ruined watchtower.

Castillo Menor

The eastern part of the castle is the oldest, having been an Iberian fortification before being controlled and further fortified by the Carthaginians then Romans. It's a strong bastion, with a Gothic entranceway, medieval battlements and some 20th-century refurbishment. Sources say that Hannibal's Iberian wife Imilce gave birth to their son in the Torre de la Reina here.

★ Top Tips

- To avoid possible 'house full' signs on busy days, buy tickets in advance on the castle website.

Take a Break

Perfectly located inside the castle gates, with a lovely large terrace, **Talaia del Castell** (www.talaiadelcastell.es) serves tapas, big morning *bocadillos*, a set lunch and some à la carte dishes.

★ Getting There

From Valencia's Estación del Norte, *cercanías* trains (€4.35, one hour) run to Xàtiva half-hourly or hourly.

It's a pleasant but long uphill walk to the castle – 2km from the centre, 2.7km from the train station. There's a taxi stand at the station.

You can drive up to the castle, where there's parking for about 25 cars, any day except Sunday. On Sundays get a shuttle bus from Plaza Españoleta in town.

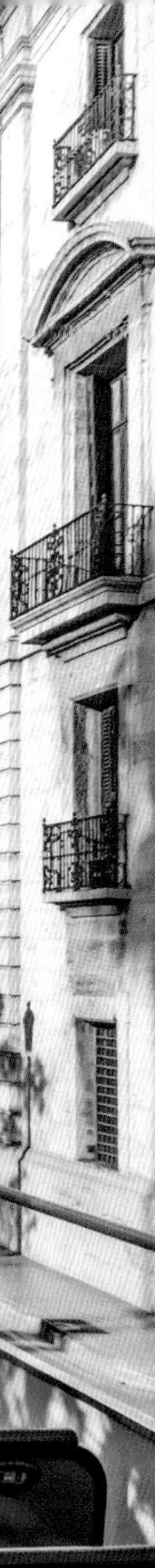

Survival Guide

Tourist bus, Valencia FRIMUFILMS/SHUTTERSTOCK ©

Before You Go

Book Your Stay

- Valencia has a good range of hotels, with a growing number of central boutique choices.
- There's a huge quantity of central apartments, which are overwhelming some districts completely. Locals complain many lack appropriate permissions.

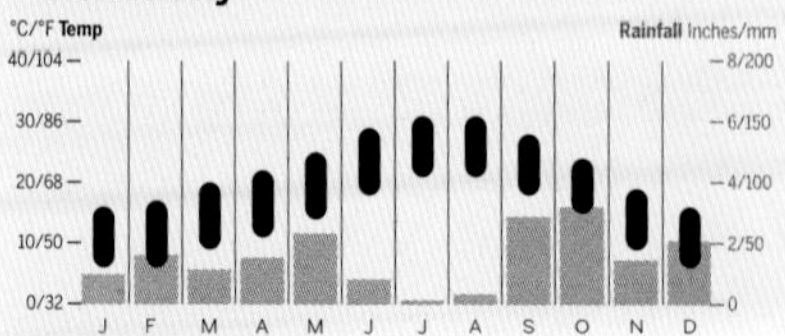

When to Go

Spring (Mar–May) Wonderful time to visit, with good but not oppressive weather, the staggering Las Fallas festival and more.

Summer (Jun–Aug) Hot but enjoyable, with lots of action in the beachfront area and hedonism in the air.

Autumn (Sep–Nov) Temperatures are still normally very pleasant, and the crowds have dropped off.

Winter (Dec–Feb) Valencia's cold season isn't cold by European standards, so don't be put off visiting then.

Best Budget

Home Youth Hostel (www.homehostelsvalencia.com) Opposite the Lonja, with top facilities.

Cantagua Hostel (www.cantaguahostel.com) Quiet, relaxed hostel on the edge of Russafa.

Purple Nest Hostel www.nesthostelsvalencia.com) Social hostel near the Turia gardens with lots of activities.

Red Nest Hostel (www.nesthostelsvalencia.com) Cheerful, modern, social nest.

Best Midrange

Hostal Antigua Morellana (www.hostalam.com) Family-run old-town spot offering great value.

Yours (www.thisisyours.es) Popular Nordic-vibe boutique hotel in Russafa.

Hotel Sorolla Centro (www.hotelrhsorollacentro.com) Top value in a winningly central spot without traffic.

Ad Hoc Carmen (www.adhochoteles.com) Handsome modern rooms with an ideal old-town location.

Best Top End

Caro Hotel (www.carohotel.com) Valencia's most enchanting hotel sits on archaeological remains.

One Shot Mercat 09 (www.hoteloneshotmercat09.com) Near the Mercado Central, this personal, intimate place is a Valencia standout.

Marqués House (www.marqueshouse.com) Modern style in a central historic building.

Hotel Balandret (www.balandret.com) Stylish boutique beach hotel.

Arriving in Valencia

Aeropuerto de Valencia (Manises)

Metro lines 3 and 5 connect the airport with central Valencia. A taxi to the city centre costs €25 to €30. The return journey is around €15 to €20.

Estación Joaquín Sorolla

Fast trains from Madrid and Barcelona arrive here. A free shuttle bus runs every few minutes to nearby Estación del Norte, which serves local trains and some slower long-distance trains. A taxi to the centre costs €4 to €7.

Estación de Autobuses

The bus station is 1km northwest of the old town. Turia metro station is a block away, and bus C2 runs to L'Eixample and Russafa. A taxi to the centre costs €4 to €7.

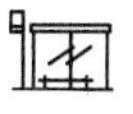

Getting Around

Public Transport

- Valencia has an integrated metro, tram and bus network.
- Metro lines (www.metrovalencia.es) cross town and serve the outer suburbs. The closest stations to the city centre are Xàtiva, Colón and Pont de Fusta.
- Metro lines 4, 6, 8 and 10 are trams – a pleasant way to get to the beach and port. Pick up the tram at Pont de Fusta station or where it intersects with the metro at Benimaclet or Marítim.
- Metro and tram rides cost €1.50/2.80/4.80 for one/two/three zones. Most rides (except to/from the airport) are single-zone. Before your first journey, you will need to buy a €2 card at the station and charge it with the number of trips you want. Allow time!
- Most buses (www.emtvalencia.es) run until about 10.30pm. Various night services continue until 1.30am (3am at weekends). Pay in cash as you get on (€1.50), or buy a **Bonobús** (€8.50 for 10 bus journeys) or **SUMA 10** (€8 for 10 bus, metro or tram rides; €20 including the airport) card at tobacconists or newspaper kiosks (or metro stations for the SUMA). The EMT website and app have journey planners.
- One-/two-/three-day travel cards (SUMA T-1/T-2/T-3) valid for buses, metro and trams cost €4/6.70/9.70, or €8/10/12 including the airport.

Bicycle

- Some bike-hire outfits also hire e-scooters and e-bikes. A four-hour rental costs around €7/15/20 for a bike/e-bike/e-scooter.

Walking Valencia

Central Valencia is compact and very walkable. Much of the old town is pedestrianised. The Turia riverbed parklands are a pleasure to walk, and a 2.5km promenade lines the city beaches.

Cycling Valencia

Valencia is a great city to cycle. It's flat, with some 160km of bike lanes. Its extensive network of *ciclocalles* (cycle streets) include the whole historic centre, where bikes have priority over cars. There are loads of bike-hire places, especially in the old town. And it has the Turia riverbed – a joy to ride.

- Many bike-hire firms offer city tours, or bike-and-boat outings to La Albufera.
- **Valenbisi** (www.valenbisi.es) is the city-bike scheme, with 300 docking stations – sign up for a weeklong contract (€13.30) on its website or app.

Bike-hire options:

Brisa (www.brisavalencia.es; Calle En Llopis 1)

Do You Bike (www.doyoubike.com; Calle de la Sangre 9)

Go VLC (www.govlc.es; Calle de Cuba 65)

Passion Bike (www.passionbike.net; Calle de Serranos 16)

Solution Bike (www.solutionbike.com; Calle Hiedra 5)

Valencia Bikes (www.valenciabikes.com; Paseo de la Pechina 32)

Taxi

- Taxis are plentiful and cheap.
- Think €10 from the centre to the beach, or €8 to the Ciudad de las Artes y las Ciencias.
- There's a minimum charge of €4 (€6 at night).
- **Radio Taxi Valencia** (☎963 70 33 33; www.radiotaxivalencia.es) and **Tele Taxi Valencia** (☎963 57 13 13; www.teletaxivalencia.com) are two of several companies.
- **PideTaxi** is a useful taxi-booking app.
- **Cabify** and **Free Now** app-based ride-share schemes operate here.

Car & Motorcycle

- Street parking is a pain.
- Nonresident vehicles are banned from most of the Barrio del Carmen.
- The cheapest central underground car park is at the corner of Avenida Oeste and Calle del Hospital.
- Numerous car-hire firms operate from the airport and city centre.

Essential Information

Accessible Travel

- Most sights, many hotels and most public institutions have wheelchair access. Most buses have descending ramps and Navilens technology to assist blind travellers. All metro stations except València Sud have adapted routes with ramps and lifts.
- Find accessibility information at www.visitvalencia.com/en/valencia-accesible.
- Valencia's city beaches and Pinedo and El Saler to the south have ramps and special boardwalks for wheelchairs to reach the water, adapted toilets, and amphibious wheelchairs and crutches.
- Boat jetties at Mirador del Pujol on La Albufera have access ramps.

Business Hours

Typical opening hours:

Banks 8.30am–2.30pm Monday to Friday

Restaurants 1pm–

3.30pm and 8pm–10.30pm; most close once a week and often Sunday evenings

Shops 10am–2pm and 5pm–8pm Monday to Friday, 10am–2pm Saturday

Bars 5pm–1.30am, to 3.30am Friday and Saturday nights

Clubs 11pm–6am Thursday to Saturday

COVID-19

Information on any travel restrictions as well as local regulations can be found at www.visitvalencia.com/en/new-normal-arrives-valencia.

Discount Cards

- **Valencia Tourist Card** (www.visitvalencia.com/valencia-tourist-card; 24/48/72hr €15/20/25) is worthwhile if you'll be busy and using public transport. It gives free travel on city public transport, free entry to 24 museums and monuments, and discounts of 10% or more at many sights, tours, bike-hire places and some shops and restaurants.
- Buy the card at tourist offices, vending machines or digital kiosks at the airport, and some hotels and newsstands.

Electricity

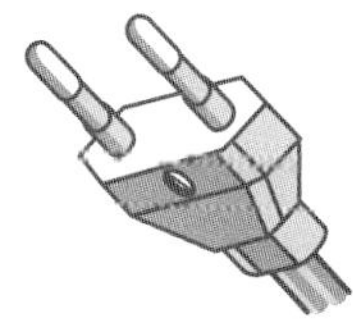

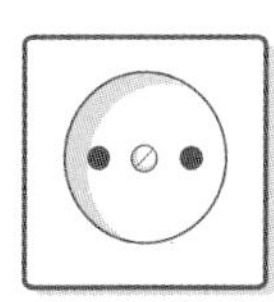

Type C
220V/50Hz

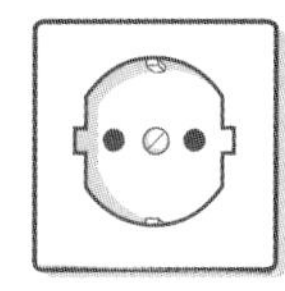

Type F
230V/50Hz

Emergency

- **General emergency number:** 112
- **Police:** 091

Money

- Spain uses the euro (€), divided into 100 céntimos.
- Credit and bank cards are widely accepted.

Tipping

Bars Locals rarely tip, though you may leave a coin or two for table service.

Hotels Not customary. A euro or two for carrying bags is appreciated.

Restaurants Not obligatory. Round up or tip up to 5%.

Taxis Not expected but many locals round up to the next euro.

Public Holidays

The two main periods when Spaniards go on holiday are Semana Santa (the week leading up to Easter Sunday) and during July and August.

The following are public holidays in Valencia.

Año Nuevo (New Year's Day) 1 January

Epifanía (Epiphany) 6 January

San Vicente Mártir (Feast of St Vincent the Martyr) 22 January

San José (Feast of St Joseph) 19 March

Viernes Santo (Good Friday) March/April

Lunes de Pascua (Easter Monday) March/April

San Vicente (Feast of St Vincent) 25 April

Fiesta del Trabajo (Labour Day) 1 May

San Juan (Feast of St John) 24 June

La Asunción (Feast of the Assumption) 15 August

Día de la Hispanidad (National Day) 12 October

Todos los Santos (All Saints Day) 1 November

Día de la Constitución (Constitution Day) 6 December

La Inmaculada Concepción (Feast of the Immaculate Conception) 8 December

Navidad (Christmas) 25 December

Safe Travel

Valencia is a safe city and you are unlikely to have any problems.

- There's a small amount of pickpocketing at major fiestas.
- Theft of unattended belongings at the beach sometimes occurs.
- Lock your bike.

Telephone Services

- International access code: 00
- Spain country code: 34
- Spain has no local area codes: landline numbers (normally starting with 9) and mobile numbers (usually starting with 6) are all nine digits.
- Roaming charges within the EU have been abolished.
- Some non-EU phone contracts include free roaming in the EU. Ask your phone provider about possible charges.
- Local SIM cards, from phone shops in Spain, can be used in unlocked phones. An e-sim with data is a good option.
- You'll need your passport to open a mobile-phone account.

Tourist Information

The city's comprehensive tourism website is www.visitvalencia.com. There is a tourist office at the airport and a few around the city.

Ayuntamiento Tourist Office (Plaza del Ayuntamiento 1) In the city hall.

Joaquín Sorolla Station Tourist Office (Estación Joaquín Sorolla)

Paz Tourist Office (Calle de la Paz 48)

Visas

Citizens of EU & Schengen countries No visa required.

Citizens of the UK, USA and most other countries not requiring an EU visa From late 2023, nationals of these countries will require pre-authorisation to enter Spain under the new European Travel Information & Authorisation System (ETIAS; www.etiasvisa.com; adult/child €7/free; valid three years). It will allow travellers to stay visa-free for 90 days within a 180-day period.

Other countries Check with a Spanish embassy or consulate.

Language

Spanish (*español*) – often referred to as *castellano* (Castilian) to distinguish it from other languages spoken in Spain – is one of the languages of Valencia. The other is *valenciano* and, while you'll find an increasing number of locals who speak *valenciano*, you will be able to get by with standard *español*. Travellers who learn a little Spanish will be amply rewarded as Spaniards appreciate the effort, no matter how basic your understanding of the language.

Just read our pronunciation guides as if they were English and you'll be understood. Note that (m/f) indicates masculine and feminine forms.

To enhance your trip with a phrasebook, visit **lonelyplanet.com**. Lonely Planet iPhone phrasebooks are available through the Apple App store.

Basics

Hello.
Hola. — o·la

Goodbye.
Adiós. — a·*dyos*

How are you?
¿Qué tal? — ke tal

Fine, thanks.
Bien, gracias. — byen *gra*·thyas

Please.
Por favor. — por fa·*vor*

Thank you.
Gracias. — *gra*·thyas

Excuse me.
Perdón. — per·*don*

Sorry.
Lo siento. — lo *syen*·to

Yes./No.
Sí./No. — *see*/*no*

Do you speak (English)?
¿Habla (inglés)? — *a*·bla (een·*gles*)

I (don't) understand.
Yo (no) entiendo. — yo (no) en·*tyen*·do

Eating & Drinking

I'm a vegetarian. (m/f)
Soy vegetariano/a. — soy ve·khe·ta·*rya*·no/a

Cheers!
¡Salud! — sa·*loo*

That was delicious!
¡Estaba buenísimo! — es·*ta*·ba bwe·*nee*·see·mo

Please bring the bill.
Por favor nos trae la cuenta. — por fa·*vor* nos *tra*·e la *kwen*·ta

I'd like ...
Quisiera ... — kee·*sye*·ra ...

a coffee	*un café*	oon ka·*fe*
a table for two	*una mesa para dos*	oo·na *me*·sa *pa*·ra dos
a wine	*un vino*	oon *vee*·no
two beers	*dos cervezas*	dos ther·*ve*·thas

Shopping

I'd like to buy ...
Quisiera comprar ... — kee·*sye*·ra kom·*prar* ...

May I look at it?
¿Puedo verlo? — *pwe*·do *ver*·lo

How much is it?
¿Cuánto cuesta? kwan·to kwes·ta

That's too/very expensive.
Es muy caro. es mooy ka·ro

Emergencies

Help!
¡Socorro! so·ko·ro

Call a doctor!
¡Llame a un médico! lya·me a oon me·dee·ko

Call the police!
¡Llame a la policía! lya·me a la po·lee·thee·a

I'm lost. (m/f)
Estoy perdido/a. es·toy per·dee·do/a

I'm ill. (m/f)
Estoy enfermo/a. es·toy en·fer·mo/a

Where are the toilets?
¿Dónde están los baños? don·de es·tan los ba·nyos

Time & Numbers

What time is it?
¿Qué hora es? ke o·ra es

It's (10) o'clock.
Son (las diez). son (las dyeth)

morning	*mañana*	ma·nya·na
afternoon	*tarde*	tar·de
evening	*noche*	no·che
yesterday	*ayer*	a·yer
today	*hoy*	oy
tomorrow	*mañana*	ma·nya·na

1	*uno*	oo·no
2	*dos*	dos
3	*tres*	tres
4	*cuatro*	kwa·tro
5	*cinco*	theen·ko
6	*seis*	seys
7	*siete*	sye·te
8	*ocho*	o·cho
9	*nueve*	nwe·ve
10	*diez*	dyeth

Transport & Directions

Where's ...?
¿Dónde está ...? don·de es·ta ...

What's the address?
¿Cuál es la dirección? kwal es la dee·rek·thyon

Can you show me (on the map)?
¿Me lo puede indicar (en el mapa)? me lo pwe·de een·dee·kar (en el ma·pa)

I want to go to ...
Quisiera ir a ... kee·sye·ra eer a ...

What time does it arrive/leave?
¿A qué hora llega/sale? a ke o·ra lye·ga/sa·le

I want to get off here.
Quiero bajarme aquí. kye·ro ba·khar·me a·kee

Behind the Scenes

Send Us Your Feedback

We love to hear from travellers – your comments help make our books better. We read every word, and we guarantee that your feedback goes straight to the authors. Visit **lonelyplanet.com/contact** to submit your updates and suggestions.

Note: We may edit, reproduce and incorporate your comments in Lonely Planet products such as guidebooks, websites and digital products, so let us know if you don't want your comments reproduced or your name acknowledged. For a copy of our privacy policy visit lonelyplanet.com/legal.

John's Thanks

Thanks above all for absolutely invaluable practical help, moral support and restorative beers to Miles Roddis, Ingrid Roddis and Isabella Noble. Also many thanks to Marie-Pascale and Jean-Luc Jacqmin. And to Carles Dolç, Disneylexya and Joan Ruiz: a pleasure to work with all of you!

Acknowledgements

Cover photograph: Front: Plaza de la Reina, Razvan Ionut Dragomirescu/Shuttertock ©; Back: Paella, Marcos Castillo/Shuttertock ©

This Book

This 4th edition of Lonely Planet's Valencia guidebook was researched and written by John Noble. The previous two editions were written by Andy Symmington. This guidebook was produced by the following:

Commissioning Editor Angela Tinson

Product Editor Alison Killilea

Cartographer Valentina Kremenchutskaya

Book Designer Megan Cassidy

Editor Kellie Langdon

Cover Researcher Hannah Blackie

Thanks to Disneylexya, Joel Cotterell, Carlos Dolç, Joan Ruiz, Gabrielle Stefanos

Index

See also separate subindexes for:
Eating p158
Drinking p159
Entertainment p159
Shopping p159

Sights 000
Map Pages **000**

Eating

Drinking

Entertainment

Shopping

Our Writer

John Noble

John loved (and still does) England's green and pleasant Ribble valley, where he grew up, but he was never content to stay in one place for too long, so th opportunity to travel and write for Lonely Planet cam as a godsend. That was a few years ago, and John ha since authored or co-authored approximately 150 Lonely Planet guidebook e ditions covering 20-odd countries scattered across the globe. Spain has been his home base since the 1990s and he remains as excited as ever about head ing out to unfamiliar destinations, especially ones yo can explore on foot.

Published by Lonely Planet Global Limited
CRN 554153
4th edition – Mar 2023
ISBN 978 1 83869 145 5

10 9 8 7 6 5 4 3 2 1
Printed in Singapore